Everyday Miracles

Everyday Miracles

Holy Moments in a Mother's Day

DALE HANSON BOURKE

WORD PUBLISHING
Dallas · London · Sydney · Singapore

EVERYDAY MIRACLES: HOLY MOMENTS IN A MOTHER'S DAY

Scripture quotations used in this book are from The Holy Bible, New International Version (NIV). Copyright © 1973, 1978, 1984 International Bible Society.

Some of the chapters in this book appeared in part in *Today's Christian Woman* magazine and are used with permission of Christianity Today, Inc.

Library of Congress Cataloging-in-Publication Data

Bourke, Dale Hanson.
    Everyday miracles : holy moments in a mother's day / Dale Hanson Bourke.
        p.   cm.
    ISBN 0-8499-0731-4
    1. Motherhood.   2. Motherhood—Religious aspects—Christianity.
I. Title.
HQ759.B753   1989
306.874'3—dc20   89-37717
                                                              CIP

Printed in the United States of America

9 8 0 1 2 3 9   BKC   9 8 7 6 5 4 3 2 1

This book is for my sons,
Chase, who sees and feels so much,
and
Tyler, whose love of life knows no bounds.

CONTENTS

CONTENTS

ACKNOWLEDGMENTS

This book would never have been written without the help and encouragement of so many people.

I am grateful to my parents, whose love and humor made my own childhood so simple and secure, and to Grandma and Grandpa Hanson, whose faith began the thread that continues through my family.

Without my husband Tom, I would not have the strength to raise our two boys, and without his consistent support I would never be able to write down our experiences in this adventure of parenting.

I would not have dared to call myself a writer if others hadn't pushed me into it:

David Shultz, who made me write a column in *Today's Christian Woman,* and supported me through the constant fear of failure;

Ron Wilson, who first helped me believe that I might have something to offer;

Kelsey Menehan, whose own writing and editing made me try harder;

Jeannette and Harold Myra, who never missed an opportunity to bolster my confidence;

ACKNOWLEDGMENTS

Ruth Stafford Peale, who gave me a little push when I needed it most;

Marilyn Jensen, my dear friend who first suggested a book;

Marlene LeFever, whose friendship and encouragement have given loyalty a new meaning;

Rebecca Pippert, who sets such a lofty standard for communicating and is still such a down-to-earth friend;

Jill Briscoe, who refuses to be admired and in doing so makes me admire her even more;

And those who have taken the time to write to me over the years to let me know that somehow, something that I wrote helped them or made them laugh.

I am especially grateful to my friends at Word Publishing who have not just made this book possible, but have invested themselves in it and in me; to Jane Struck, whose editing deserves an award; and to Leslie Nunn, without whom I would never have the time, energy, or sanity to write.

INTRODUCTION

Somewhere among the dishes and diapers, the runny noses and carpool lines are glimpses of grace. These are the moments when God reaches into our everyday lives and—if we will let him—performs miracles. He takes muddy little hands and transforms them into instruments of love. He empowers stumbling bedtime prayers with eternal wisdom. And somedays he even makes McDonald's seem like a cathedral.

These are holy moments. They are precious and sacred and rare. And too often, in our rush to be good mothers, we forget to stop and treasure these gifts. But when we do, we are humbled by the awesome discovery that God gave us children not so much that we can teach, but so that we can learn.

I once had a photography teacher who shot what he called suburban landscapes. At first I was unimpressed with his work. It consisted of black and white photos of garbage cans, swing sets, and cookie-cutter houses.

But as I came to understand his point of view, I began to see the beauty in the photos: the symmetry of the garbage cans, the simplicity of the swing set, the subtle contrasts among the similarities of the houses.

The photos which had seemed unimpressive became works of art.

As a mother, I live those suburban landscapes. I can look at my days and see nothing but chaos, or I can stop and really appreciate them. Sometimes what I see among the clutter and confusion takes my breath away. In the midst of it all, there is a beauty that transcends the ordinary.

God speaks to some people through a majestic mountain or a perfect rose. But in my life he speaks through broken toys and handprints on my walls.

I write about what I know. These are not extraordinary events, and I am not an extraordinary mother. I lose my patience far too often. My words don't match my actions. My children are not the best behaved, and they often wear mismatched clothes.

Despite all of this, perhaps because of it, we are learning and growing and discovering more about ourselves and God each day. These discoveries are everyday miracles. Ordinary, but life-changing. Basic, but holy.

Did I see the holiness in these moments as they occurred? Sometimes. In those cases, like a photographer, I simply pointed my camera and recorded the scene. But in most cases I was just going about my life, and it took a mental replay to see the grace of a simple scene. Sometimes I did not see the lesson at all. But as I sat to write in my journal, the words came together. I would read in amazement the words that appeared on the page, just as a photographer is often surprised by the developing image.

I wrote some of these stories for my column in *Today's Christian Woman* magazine, but most I wrote because the writing itself helped me take a fresh look at my life as a mother. I have arranged them in this book roughly as the events occurred, except for the first, which is one of the most recent. As I reread some of my earliest accounts, I almost laugh at what I thought I knew. In a few years, I expect to laugh at what I am writing now.

I share these events with you because I want you to see that holy moments are there in your home, too, waiting to be appreciated. They are there every day for the taking.

Marcel Proust once said, "The real voyage of discovery consists not in seeking new landscapes, but having new eyes." I wish you new eyes to see and new ears to hear the holy moments in your own life.

1

IT WILL
CHANGE
YOUR LIFE

*T*ime is running out for my friend. We are sitting at lunch when she casually mentions that she and her husband are thinking of "starting a family." What she means is that her biological clock has begun its countdown and she is being forced to consider the prospect of motherhood.

"We're taking a survey," she says, half joking. "Do you think I should have a baby?"

"It will change your life," I say carefully, keeping my tone neutral.

"I know," she says. "No more sleeping in on Saturdays, no more spontaneous vacations . . ."

But that is not what I mean at all. I look at my friend, trying to decide what to tell her.

I want her to know what she will never learn in childbirth classes. I want to tell her that the physical wounds of childbearing heal, but that becoming a mother will leave her with an emotional wound so raw that she will be forever vulnerable.

I want to tell her that becoming a mother will leave her with an emotional wound so raw that she will be forever vulnerable.

I consider warning her that she will never read a newspaper again without asking, "What if that had been my child?" That every plane crash, every fire will haunt her. That when she sees pictures of starving children, she will look at the mothers and wonder if anything could be worse than watching your child die.

I look at her carefully manicured nails and stylish suit and think she should know that no matter how sophisticated she is, becoming a mother will immediately reduce her to the primitive level of a she-bear protecting her cub. That a slightly urgent call of "Mom!" will cause her to drop a soufflé or her best crystal without a moment's hesitation. That the anger she will feel if that call came over a lost toy will be a joy she has never before experienced.

I feel I should warn her that no matter how many years she has invested in her career, she will be professionally derailed by motherhood. She might successfully arrange for childcare, but one day she will be waiting to go into an important business meeting, and she will think about her baby's sweet smell. She will have to use every ounce of discipline to keep from running home, just to make sure he is all right.

I want my friend to know that everyday routine decisions will no longer be routine. That a visit to McDonald's and a five-year-old boy's understandable desire to go to the men's room rather than the women's will become a major dilemma. That right there, in the midst of clattering trays and screaming children, issues of independence and gender identity will be weighed against the prospect that a child molester may be lurking in the restroom. I want her to know that however decisive she may be at the office, she will second guess herself constantly as a mother.

Looking at my attractive friend, I want to assure her that eventually she will shed the pounds of pregnancy, but she will never feel the same way about herself. That her life, now so important, will be of less value to her once she has a child. That she would give it up in a moment to save her offspring, but will also begin to hope for more years, not so much to accomplish her own dreams, but to watch her child accomplish his. I want her to know that a cesarean scar or shiny stretch marks will become badges of honor.

My friend's relationship with her husband will change, I know; but not in the ways she thinks. I wish she could understand how much more you can love a man who is careful to always powder the baby or who never hesitates to play "bad guys" with his son. I think she should know that she will fall in love with her husband again for reasons she would now find very unromantic.

I wish my modern friend could sense the bond she will feel with women throughout history who have tried desperately to stop war and prejudice and drunk driving. I hope she will understand why I can think rationally about most issues, but become temporarily insane when I discuss the threat of nuclear war to my children's future.

I want to describe to my friend the exhilaration of seeing your son learn to hit a baseball. I want to capture for her the belly laugh of a baby who is touching the soft fur of a dog for the first time. I want her to taste the joy that is so real that it hurts.

My friend's quizzical look makes me realize that tears have formed in my eyes. "You'll never regret it," I say finally. Then I reach across the table, and squeezing my friend's hand, I offer a prayer for her and me and all of the mere mortal women who stumble their way into this holiest of callings.

2

TOUCHED
BY LOVE

*T*here was no getting around it. I was feeling profoundly sorry for myself as I shuffled on to the airplane that would take me home from a brief trip. Four months pregnant, I had outgrown most of my clothes, but my maternity dresses looked as if I were playing dress-up. So I made do with baggy sweaters and pinned skirts and tried to fight the nausea that still followed me into my second trimester.

I sat down with a sigh and loosened the seat belt enough to accommodate my growing middle. The seat next to me was empty except for newspapers that the man one seat over was discarding. "Mind if I look at the front page?" I asked. Maybe reading something would take my mind off of my troubles. I glanced over at the man for a moment as he said, "Help yourself."

Horned-rim glasses, neat haircut, button-down shirt, small-print tie. Must be a lawyer, I thought, as I checked off all of the telltale signs. "Interesting day for news," he said cordially as he turned the pages. I smiled, but said nothing. I just wasn't in the mood for idle chatter.

"Coffee?" the flight attendant offered. It smelled wonderful. "No thanks," I said looking at it longingly.

"I'd love some," the man with the newspaper replied cheerfully. "I just need a little help with my tray table." I glanced over to see why his table wasn't working. When he dropped his newspaper, I stared at him for a moment as I realized the problem. His table was fine. But the man's arm ended at his elbow.

The flight attendant helped him with his tray as he folded up the newspaper. "Thank you," he said, reaching for the cup with a hand that looked more like a child's. I tried not to stare. But as I glanced in the man's direction, I saw him drinking his coffee and reading the paper with surprising grace and ease.

Catching my eye, the man smiled warmly. "I thought the coffee would never come," he said. "It smells great," I replied. "I wish I could have some, but I'm pregnant and it's against the doctor's orders." *How foolish,* I thought. *Here I am, complaining about not*

*being able to drink coffee, and I'm sitting next to a man
who doesn't even have a good hand.*

But he didn't seem to notice my selfishness.
"When are you due?" he asked. We talked for a few
minutes, and I noticed how skillfully he turned the
conversation toward me. He seemed genuinely inter-
ested as I told him about my pregnancy.

"By the way, my name's Dan," he said as he held
out his misshapen hand. I introduced myself and hoped
he hadn't noticed any hesitation as I shook his hand.

"What type of business are you in?" he asked,
again easing me through an awkward moment.
"Publishing," I said. "How about you?"

"I work for a news service," he said. "I've been on
the road for the last week covering some stories." For
the next hour, Dan and I talked about everything from
our shared belief in God to our common interest in
journalism. He told me funny stories about how people
treated him because of his disability—like the man who
shouted at him, for some reason believing his hearing
was impaired. He talked about the difficulty of having
friends who sometimes felt sorry for him. He talked
about his career, and his hopes of finding an even more
challenging position.

Finally I asked him the question that had been
forming the entire time we had been talking: How was
it that he was such a whole person despite his physical
handicap?

"I grew up in a wonderful, loving, godly home,"

he explained. "My mother always told me I was special. I never realized what an advantage that was until I met people who had no physical handicaps, but were scarred forever on the inside."

❧

Looking at Dan, I knew his mother had accomplished more than most people dream of in a lifetime.

❧

"Tell me about your mother," I asked, wondering what kind of a woman could raise such an extraordinary child.

Dan smiled as he recounted boyhood memories of coming home after playing softball, crying because he had lost a game. "She was kind and caring," he said. "But she never let me use my disability as an excuse. She told me to go out and try harder the next day," he said smiling fondly. "As a child I thought that being the way I am was about like being left-handed. It was different, but not necessarily worse. It couldn't have been easy for her, I realize now," he continued. "The doctors recommended that I be institutionalized. But my mother insisted on caring for me at home.

"Some people criticized her for pushing me too hard, but she used to say, 'If I do everything for him now, who will take care of him when I am gone?'"

Looking at Dan, I knew his mother had accomplished more than most people dream of in a lifetime. Dan was a living testimony to the power of a mother's love.

As our trip came to an end, Dan picked up his bags and ran to catch another flight. I stood watching him, my hands resting on my growing stomach. I wondered what kind of mother I would be to this child. As Dan waved, I felt tears in my eyes. *"Thank you, God,"* I prayed, *"for trusting me with this child. And thank you for helping me understand just how important a mother's love can be."*

3

LESSONS
FROM
MY SON

*A*t 2:00 in the after-noon, I was finally getting around to taking my "morning" shower. The shower door was only half closed so I could listen for my week-old son's cries, and I soaped my hair fever-ishly, aware that each quiet minute might be my last.

I rinsed the soap from my hair and began to reach for my conditioner, then stopped. It was just one more luxury I couldn't afford at this stage in my life. I'd prob-ably have a headful of split ends by the time my son was a month old.

I drip-dried myself and took a quick swipe at my

hair with the blow-dryer before braiding the still soggy mass into a ponytail. No time for makeup, except for a half moon of concealer under each eye in a vain attempt to hide the sunken dark circles. I was wondering if anyone had ever died from lack of sleep when I heard the now familiar wail from the baby's room. I was on duty again.

Motherhood is not quite what I expected it to be. Oh, I knew there would be sleepless nights and dirty diapers and cries that seemed to go on forever. That's why I had taken vitamins during pregnancy, read books on childbirth and motherhood, and quizzed my obstetrician and pediatrician. I bought educational toys, read books on infant stimulation, and studied experts' opinions on childhood development. I had planned to be the ultimate informed, in-control mother.

What I hadn't counted on was a bright-eyed, active little baby with a mind of his own. His personality seemed set from birth, and he loves to defy all the theories I so carefully studied. Instead of sharing our lives with a passive, docile infant, my husband and I have been joined by an opinionated little person.

It's the fact of his full-fledged personality that astounds me most about this child of ours. Certainly his birth was a miracle. I will never forget the moment when I saw him slide out into the world, a healthy, squirming little being who had been inside of me for all those months. And I never tire of examining his perfect little fingers and toes. But the fact that he has a God-given personality already in place is the greatest miracle of all. No matter what we do as parents, there is a great deal about little Chase that we will never affect. He is his own person, and we are only his caretakers.

It is in this realization that I have learned a great deal about myself. Control is something I treasure. I like to feel that I can handle a situation, determine the outcome, measure the progress. I love setting goals and objectives, and I'm lost without my "to do" list—even on weekends. I value anything that helps me save time, become more efficient, or further organize my life.

Control does not seem to be at the top of the job description for motherhood.

Unfortunately, control does not seem to be at the top of the job description for motherhood. I can tell Chase that he's not supposed to be hungry yet, but I can't control what his stomach seems to be telling him. I can swaddle him in blankets to keep him warm, but I seem unable to control his persistent feet that can escape from the confines of any clothing or covering.

In short, there are times when I feel like a total failure because my standards of achievement are much more rigid than my son's.

And then there are those moments of totally un-earned joy when my baby smiles at me or coos or grabs my shoulder and nuzzles my neck. Those times come not because I have set a goal or completed a task, but because I am simply providing love and security for an-other human being. At no other time in my life have I felt so loved for just being me.

For years now I think God has been trying to teach me that love is not something that can be earned. Like many "achievers," I have somehow believed that accomplishing more would make me more worthy of love. Yet through the gift of my son, I am learning that I can fail by some standards and succeed by others.

My son may grow up to find a mother with per-petually dark circles under her eyes and hair like straw, but I hope he'll know that I love him more than any of my more measurable achievements. And I hope, too, that he will continue to love and accept me, even if I do nothing more than just be there when he needs me.

4

HOME IS WHERE THE HEART IS

*M*aking the rounds at a holiday party last year, I literally bumped into an attractive young woman who looked like she was alone. We went through the usual polite introductions, and then she asked me how I knew the host couple. "Business," I explained. "I do some work with Joe. What about you?"

"Oh, my husband and Joe are old college friends," she said. "I'm just a homemaker."

"How nice," I said, trying to sound positive. "Tell me what you do at home."

"What I *do?*" she said, her voice rising a bit.

"Well, I mean everyone asks people with jobs outside the home about their work and responsibilities, and I'd really like to know what your job is like."

"Well," she began slowly, "I take the kids to school and ballet classes and Little League practice, and I make the beds and do the grocery shopping and cook dinner and wash clothes and take the dog to the vet's and . . ."

She was beginning to look depressed, so I tried another tack. "I've always thought it would be great to be able to organize your time at home so that you could pursue a hobby or do some reading during the day," I ventured. "What do you do for fun?"

"Fun?" she said, looking at me as if I had two heads. "I barely have time to put on my makeup in the morning."

"Oh," I said lamely, having exhausted my curiosity about homemaking and feeling like I had irreparably alienated the woman. As we drifted away from each other and into other conversations, I couldn't help feeling a little sorry for her. After all, I was trying to be sensitive to her situation. *Why was this woman so defensive?* I wondered.

Less than a year later I have found the answer to that question. Having spent some time out of the office and in the home full time following the birth of my son, I feel like calling up that woman and telling her I understand what she was getting at.

By the end of my maternity leave I, too, was feeling a bit defensive about my life as a homemaker. It seems that everyone thought that I was on vacation or at least watching soap operas and eating bonbons all day. After all, what could I be *doing* all day at home?

One day I asked myself that question. How in the world did my day just seem to disappear into errands and cleaning up and making dinner? At the office I was often crossing off one more major task on my "to do" list by the time 5:00 P.M. rolled around. At home I was panicking over the dozens of projects I hadn't even begun.

*H*ow *in the world did my day just seem to disappear into errands and cleaning up and making dinner?*

Admittedly, I am hardly a good case in point. I've spent most of my life in an office rather than the home, and I was ill equipped to deal with most situations that experienced homemakers handle every day. But I was also astonished that people treated me differently in my role as homemaker than I was used to being treated at the office. At times it was subtle, at other times more obvious. But all in all, it came down to an attitude that a woman who works at home isn't busy, while a woman in a business suit is. Therefore, the homemaker is free to run one more errand, do one more favor, or listen to one more story. A woman who works outside the home always seems to have more important things to do.

The principle behind all this seems to be that at the office time is money. At home, time tends to be people. And in an economically oriented society, the value of that people time isn't always easy to calculate. There are few yardsticks for measuring growth in people rather than earnings.

What can be done to remedy the situation? Not much as long as we live in a society that believes money makes the world go 'round. We can probably only make a difference as individuals and in the way we respond to the role of homemaking.

Now that I'm back in the business world, I rarely ask a homemaker what she *does* anymore. Instead, I ask her to tell me about her children, or her neighborhood, or her church. And in response to those kinds of questions, her face often lights up and her answers are warm and lively—because it's in those spheres that she is making the world go 'round. And now I know just how difficult her job really is.

5

THE
WONDERS
OF THE
WORLD

I always wanted to see the world. Travel to exotic places. Explore new sights. Experience unknown adventures. Every month I would pour over *Travel and Leisure* and dream of places like Marrakech, Maracaibo, and Manila. I imagined myself scaling the Great Wall of China or shopping in some Middle Eastern bazaar.

Then one day my dreams came true. I was given a passport and an open-ended ticket and embarked upon an adventure into an entirely new world. Well, not exactly a *new* world, but a world I had never seen before. A world of wonder and adventure and sights as exotic as I had ever imagined.

The world I'm exploring these days has never been detailed in travel guides, so I have to rely on a trusted tour guide to show me the way. Every day he takes me by the hand and points out new discoveries while we ooh and aah together.

Just this morning we discovered the way light shines on the leaf of a philodendron. And yesterday we explored every nook on the underside of our dining room table. My son, the two-foot-tall explorer, is sharing his world with me.

I'm wearing out the knees of my pants on my daily adventures with Chase. But it's a small price to pay for what I'm learning about his world and mine. We're enjoying the wonder of water as we splash it, taste it, and watch it run down our noses. We've tried to grab shadows and touch the people on television. We've chased ice cubes across the floor and found that radiators are sometimes cool, but sometimes hot. We've tasted ice cream and apples and vitamins. (We both prefer ice cream.)

Sometimes I think I am more awed by this experience than my son is. For thirty years I've been learning to be nonchalant, unruffled, and poised about the world in which I live. Then along came this little guy and dissolved the facade. Now I roll around on the floor, make funny noises, and giggle with him over silly little games.

I'm not sure when I first lost my own sense of wonder. I do remember that as a teenager it was very important to be "cool." My girlfriends and I spent hours perfecting a nonchalant walk, an appropriate slouch, and a casual flip of our hair. It was all designed to make us look like we didn't really care. It wasn't cool at all to look like you were trying. I suppose that was when I started to lose my ability to appreciate the world around me.

Perhaps now, for the first time in a long time, I can understand what Christ meant when he said we must become like little children.

As a young woman in the business world, I worked hard to appear in control and unruffled. I was afraid that I looked as young and naive as I felt, so I dressed in high heels and suits and hoped someone would take me seriously. No matter how surprised I was by people or circumstances, I always acted casual.

For as long as I can remember, I wanted to appear sophisticated—to seem more cosmopolitan than my small-town roots implied. I wanted to be well-read, informed, and worldly-wise.

There's probably nothing inherently wrong with those aspirations, but I can see now that they lead me to close myself off at times. I learned to control my sense of wonder. I came to expect that only exotic places would stimulate my curiosity.

Perhaps now, for the first time in a long time, I can understand what Christ meant when he said we must become like little children. I'm discovering that for Christians, being cool is not so cool after all. Being open and vulnerable and awed by God's love and his creation are truly valuable traits.

I still subscribe to *Travel and Leisure* and file away articles about faraway lands, but my perspective has changed. Maybe I'll travel more when my husband and I retire. For now I'm just busy feeling the smooth surface of a leaf and learning to say ooh and aah all over again.

6

LONG-TERM
INVESTMENTS

We were five minutes into a five-hour flight and my eighteen-month-old son had already grown bored with all of his toys. After scattering the contents of my purse, he began deftly dismantling the airplane's interior.

Suddenly his attention was focused on the woman in the seat next to mine, who was about to put on her earphones. As he grabbed for the headset, I made an attempt to restrain him, bringing on howls and a look that said, "You never let me have any fun!"

I began my well-practiced litany of apologies to

the woman and promised that once the seat belt sign was turned off, my son and I would lock ourselves in the bathroom for the rest of the flight.

"Oh, it's all right," she assured me. "I was really enjoying watching you two. It's obvious that you love him very much."

"I *do* love him," I replied. "But I can't believe it shows at a time like this." As I said the words, Chase lunged at my earrings, taking them off my ears and holding up his prize with a smile. "He's really a handful," I added lamely.

"I guess I was like that as a kid, too," the woman said. "But no one really took the time to care about what I did."

In between dashes up and down the aisles as I followed my son, the woman and I struck up a conversation about the weather, the news, and her own childhood. Slowly the story of her early life unfolded. Her parents had divorced while she was an infant. Her father was too busy with his career to even visit, and her mother eventually became an alcoholic. Unable to care for her children, the woman was forced to give them over to the state to be sent to foster homes.

The young woman's childhood had been a jumble of experiences. Shuttled from one home to another, she was mistreated and abused in some and reminded she "didn't really belong" in others. By the time she was fifteen she had become withdrawn, sullen, and was labeled a troublemaker.

But then she entered a home that was different from the others. She was given a room of her own. Her foster mother bought her nice clothes and told her how pretty she looked. Slowly she won the girl's trust and gave back compassion and the loving discipline that had been missing in the girl's life.

Ten years later this girl was sitting next to me on the airplane, looking like the successful career woman that she was. "The fact that I am normal at all is because of that one woman who cared enough to love a troublemaker," she told me with tears in her eyes.

Now the pace of motherhood often frustrated my work ethic mentality, making me wonder if I was getting enough done or if life was passing me by.

I thought of that foster mother and wondered where she'd found the courage to take in that teenager, the strength to love her, and the humility to invest hours in a cause that would earn her no awards or recognition. "She must be very special," I said, knowing that it had taken superhuman grace to accomplish such a miracle.

For the rest of the flight, I played with my son and realized that my earlier frustrations had disappeared. I watched him explore and marveled at his curiosity. I listened to his laugh and envied his enjoyment of life. When he threw his arms around me in a spontaneous hug, I held him until he squirmed out of my arms, intent on new discoveries.

I remembered the many times I had spent alone on flights in the past, carrying a briefcase instead of a diaper bag, trying to accomplish as much as possible before I dashed off the airplane to my next business meeting. Now the pace of motherhood often frustrated my work ethic mentality, making me wonder if I was getting enough done or if life was passing me by.

But the story I had just heard reminded me that many of life's most valuable investments have much more long-term returns. *"Please God,"* I prayed as I walked off the airplane, *"don't let me settle for achievements when I could help shape a life."*

7

FORGIVE US OUR SINS

y son has always been slightly precocious, and true to form, he entered the "terrible twos" a full week before his second birthday. Normally I'm proud of his early accomplishments. I note them in his baby book, just in case he becomes famous some day and I'm interviewed about his early patterns of achievement. But I would have gladly entered this phase behind schedule.

One day he was a sweet, loving baby who liked to give me hugs and kisses and gladly picked up his toys. Then, on a Saturday in July, he was transformed into a foot-stomping, toy-throwing, food-spitting little boy whose favorite (and sometimes only) word was "No!"

On this memorable day, my son and I set out to do our grocery shopping, which had, up until that point, been a pleasant routine for both of us. As I started to place Chase in the seat of the shopping cart, he began to kick his feet and say, "No, I push."

"Don't be silly, Honey," I said in my best maternal voice. "Mommy pushes and Chase sits in the seat."

"No!" he shrieked as other shoppers began to look our way. Feeling like one-of-those-mothers-who-can't-control-her-child, I patiently reasoned, coaxed, and threatened my son into the seat. As we rolled through the aisles, I found myself grabbing for items with one hand and using my other hand to keep him firmly planted in the cart. As the cart filled, he seemed to relax a bit, and I (foolishly) let down my guard. I looked up from the freezer section to see my son twisted around in his seat, grabbing items out of our basket and dumping them onto the floor.

Nearly at the end of my list—and patience—I rolled Chase into the produce section and madly grabbed at salad ingredients. In the middle of my search for a ripe tomato, I turned around to find Chase taking a bite out of a cucumber. "But you don't even like vegetables," I heard myself say, and Chase, agreeing, spat out the bite onto his shirt.

As we checked out, the man who was packing our groceries said, "Spare the rod and spoil the child.

Remember those words, lady. It worked for me with my ten kids." I began to explain that I believed in the same philosophy when Chase started to squirm in my arms and point at the Pac-Man machine. "No, we're going home now," I said firmly. My attempt to demonstrate discipline was greeted with howls. I hurriedly made my exit, juggling groceries and my whining child.

The miracle of Christ's forgiveness never seemed so understandable to me as the day Chase first said, "I sorry."

"All right, Chase, this is it," I said when we got home. "You're going to have your lunch now, and then you'll take your nap." I was convinced that Chase's changed behavior was the result of my spoiling him. I needed to get the situation under control before he became a juvenile delinquent.

I wrestled him into his highchair, handed him his

spoon, and offered him his lunch. Just then the telephone rang, and as I turned to answer it, I heard a crash. There sat Chase, my once sweet child, with food spattered all over him and the floor.

"Chase Hanson Bourke, you're in trouble!" I said, drawing on the memory of the voice my mother had once used on me. As I grabbed the paper towels and stamped toward him, he looked up at me, and in a quiet voice said, "I sorry." I don't know where he'd learned to say it. It was certainly the first time I'd heard it. But by the look of utter repentance on his face, I knew he understood the words. And, perhaps for the first time, I understood them, too.

For as my son sat in his highchair with food spattered on him, all I saw was the look in his eyes that seemed to ask, "Do you still love me?" And despite the accumulated frustrations of the morning, all I felt was a wave of emotion that brought tears to my eyes.

I hugged Chase, food in his hair and all, and assured him of my forgiveness. Then I said a quick prayer of thanksgiving, not just for the gift of my son, but also for the lessons I continue to learn from him.

I don't know how many times in my life I have said, "I'm sorry." Certainly some of my apologies have come easier than others. Sometimes the words haven't been able to erase the devastation I've caused. Other times they've come so easily that they've merely punctuated a conversation and helped it flow more smoothly. But the concept of being forgiven—especially by God—has always been difficult for me to understand.

How could God really forgive me when day in and day out I manage to bungle things so badly, forgetting lessons learned and regressing to my selfish instincts? How could he truly love me despite my constant misbehavior?

Yet the miracle of Christ's forgiveness never seemed so understandable to me as the day Chase first said, "I sorry." I forgave him quickly and wholeheartedly. I joyously cleaned up the mess and patiently put him down for his nap.

It wasn't that I expected him to suddenly reform. I knew that we would be living through the "terrible twos" for a while. But it was enough for me that he uttered the words and meant them. And as I forgave my son, I seemed to hear my Father say, "*Yes, my daughter, I will continue to forgive you, too.*"

8

HOLIDAY MEMORIES

A friend of mine and I were discussing the importance of holiday traditions recently. Both new to the art of mothering, we were suddenly feeling the pressure to establish traditions for our families "before it was too late." After all, we both had young sons who, we were told, needed meaningful holidays as much as they needed play groups, snug-fitting diapers, and educational toys. Who knew what would happen to our toddlers if we didn't provide the right environment? Would they be ostracized in grade school? Would they grow up and confess to psychological abuse in their formative years?

As the holidays approached, I began taking this task quite seriously—reading books, studying expert advice, listening to "successful" mothers—when it suddenly occurred to me that my own holidays had been nearly traditionless.

To say my family *always* did things one way would be to deny the essentially spontaneous nature of the Hansons. We never let one celebration serve as precedent for the next. We rarely followed a path we'd walked before. In fact, my memories of holidays are a crazy quilt of sights, sounds, and activities—few tied to one another.

There was the Thanksgiving that we were in the midst of moving and my mother served a turkey roll in the center of her large, handpainted platter. Sitting among the boxes, we laughed until we cried at the sight of the pitiful little processed bird. And there was the year we had our Thanksgiving lunch at a hot dog stand so that we could travel to both grandparents' houses in one day and keep peace among the relatives.

There was the Christmas that my parents let me open "just one gift" on Christmas Eve. Knowing my essentially greedy nature, they counted on my choosing the largest box, which they had filled with nuts. Although we had a good laugh, they sensed my disappointment, and let me open the rest of my presents that night.

And then there was the Christmas morning that the presents arrived in the shower stall. We had no fireplace, so my father explained, with an almost straight face, that Santa must have lost weight and squeezed through the faucet to deliver the gifts.

I suppose, after reviewing my memories, that there was *one* holiday tradition in my family. The tradition was humor, and it had a way of wrapping itself around all the diverse activities of holidays and other times of the year. It got us through turkey rolls and hot dogs, unexpected presents, and houses without fireplaces. It made our Christmas tree sparkle and gave us moments of joy when we least expected them.

If there was one thing we were always able to do, it was to laugh at ourselves and even at each other.

It salved the wounds of childhood, too, and eased me through skinned knees, the deaths of pets, and the disappointments of friendships. It put sibling rivalries in perspective and gave me confidence that I belonged.

If there was one thing we were always able to do, it was to laugh at ourselves and even at each other.

Sometimes one of us took it personally and had to be lovingly teased back into the fold, but mostly we all knew that no matter what, we were part of one crazy, loving family. Even if we celebrated holidays erratically or treated tradition irreverently, we still knew that family times were special.

So as I prepare my own young family for the holidays, I'm becoming more relaxed about establishing traditions. My son can probably enjoy the holidays without a special menu, a keepsake ornament, or a carefully trimmed tree. But I don't think he can truly appreciate any holiday without love and humor.

9

A CHILD SHALL LEAD THEM

The sun was just coming up as we entered Los Angeles International Airport. I was carrying a small suitcase, and my young son wore a toy-filled backpack decorated with ducks. We were headed home after a week in California.

We're beginning to get the hang of this, I thought a bit smugly as Chase and I wound our way through the airport and into the check-in line. Since my son's birth, we had traveled together whenever possible. At times the logistics seemed overwhelming; changing diapers, warming bottles, and amusing an active two-year-old

within the confines of an airplane could be a monu-
mental task.

But right from the start, Chase loved the adventure of it all, and now we negotiated airports together
like pros.

"I'm sorry, ma'am, but that flight has been can-
celed," the man said as he took our tickets. "However,
I can put you on our next flight to Denver that leaves
in two hours. Then you can change planes in
Chicago. . . ."

As the ticket agent explained the new route that
would zigzag us across the country over the next twelve
hours, I looked at my son and felt my confidence dis-
solve. "There's got to be something else," I said ur-
gently. "Doesn't any other airline fly to Washington?"

"Well," the man said, after staring at his computer
for several minutes, "our competition has a nonstop
flight leaving in the next hour, but you'd have to go all
the way to the last terminal. I don't think you can make
it in time."

"Could you please book us on it?" Barely waiting
for his nod, I gathered up our belongings, and we took
off running.

After a mad dash, we made it to the other terminal. But when I presented our tickets again, explaining
we had been rescheduled on the new flight, the reser-
vationist apologized. "I'm sorry, but we don't have any
reservations for you. The agent at the other airline
must not have called them in."

I must have looked like I was about to cry, because

the woman gave me an encouraging smile and added, "Let's see what we can do."

The flight was already full, but as we waited and she punched buttons, two seats miraculously opened. "We got you on!" she said excitedly. "But you'll have to hurry. The flight's about to leave."

Thanking her, we rushed down the long hall to our airplane. At last we spotted our gate and the blinking light indicating the plane was already boarding. We rushed ahead only to be stopped by a group of people wearing tattered clothes, huddled in the boarding area. They didn't seem to be moving toward the airplane.

"Excuse me," I said.

"'scuse me," Chase mimicked.

But neither of our requests received attention from the group. Finally, a woman from the airline herded the group to the side and motioned for us to pass. "They're from Cambodia," she explained. "They don't speak English."

As we passed the group, I noticed that despite the California heat, they all wore heavy coats. Still, they seemed to huddle together as if for warmth.

We walked on to the airplane and made our way to the back, finding our seats in the middle of the smoking section. "Oh, great. We're stuck behind a kid," the man behind me said to his wife. I resisted the urge to give him a dirty look and concentrated instead on getting Chase settled in his seat.

Just as we fastened our seat belts, the group of people we had seen earlier were escorted down the aisle.

The flight attendant pointed them toward seats across from ours. As they sat down, I realized that they were part of an extended family: mother, father, two boys, and their grandmother.

They seemed nervous and tired, and they sat in their seats without removing their coats or storing the shopping bags each carried. I realized then that all their possessions were either in their bags or on their backs, and they were afraid to part with anything.

I watched with tears in my eyes as my son took his cherished train and handed it to the two boys, who seemed to understand the value of the gift.

My attention turned back to my son as he proclaimed, "Look, Mommy, a movie," pointing at the safety film that was playing on the airplane's screen.

"Let's talk quietly," I urged, not wanting to give the man behind me any more reason to dislike children.

"Okay," Chase whispered, then in total delight shrieked, "A teddy bear! That boy in the movie has a teddy bear!" Sure enough, my eagle-eyed son had spotted the one toy in the entire safety film and wanted everyone to share his discovery.

I heard the man behind me swear about children and "smelly foreigners," and I bit my lip as I thought of all the people in the world who must offend him.

Take-off occupied our attention for the next few minutes. As soon as the seat belt light went off, Chase was ready to empty his backpack and begin playing with his toys. "My train. Where's my train?" he asked, panic creeping into his voice. His little plastic train had become his favorite possession over the past weeks, and whenever it was out of sight for more than a few minutes he became frantic. He even slept with it in his crib.

But his trains were safely packed in my purse along with our tickets, and Chase squealed again as he saw them. We played with the trains and his other toys for the next hour, trying to ignore the smoke that surrounded us and the ever-grumbling man behind me. I had forgotten all about the Cambodian family until I looked up and saw two pairs of big brown eyes watching Chase play with his toys. I realized that the two little boys had sat quietly for the past hour without anything to amuse them. I thought of the four hours left in their long journey, and my heart went out to the young boys, one my son's age and the other a little older.

"Chase," I said, "those little boys don't have any toys and you have so many."

"Their toys are in their suitcase," he said matter-of-factly.

"No," I explained, "they don't have any toys at all." Chase looked at me skeptically.

"Not even at home?" he asked, beginning to understand the seriousness of the situation. Chase was good about sharing toys with his playmates, but he lived in a world of privileged children. So the thought of no toys—not even at home—was new to Chase.

"Maybe you could let the boys play with some of your toys," I nudged.

At first Chase pretended not to hear me, but I knew it was his way of thinking through a decision. "All right, Mommy," he said, less than enthusiastically. Then looking at me with wide eyes he asked, "Do I have to let them play with my train?"

"No, Chase," I assured him. Relieved, he carefully picked out two Matchbox race cars, marched across the airplane aisle, and ceremoniously presented each car to the little boys who looked surprised and then thrilled. The boys' mother looked at me with a grateful smile, the grandmother patted Chase on the head, and the little boys grinned and bobbed their heads up and down to show their thanks for the cars they were holding carefully.

My own son turned and looked at me with a big smile. "They like them, Mommy," he said excitedly. Then soberly, "They don't have *any* toys, not even at home." And after glancing at them one more time, he looked at me and said, "They can have my train, too."

I watched with tears in my eyes as my son took his cherished train and handed it to the two boys, who seemed to understand the value of the gift. From behind me, I heard the familiar gruff voice say, "You've got a fine little boy there." I smiled at the man, then leaned over to give my son a hug. He struggled out of my arms and back to his toys, oblivious to the sacred drama in which he had just played a starring role.

The rest of the flight went quickly. I watched Chase play, and silently thanked God for the cancellations and confusion that had led us to two seats in the middle of the smoking section on a crowded airplane.

"*A little child shall lead them.*" As these words ran through my mind, I realized that God could use one small gesture to welcome a family of pilgrims, open the eyes of a bigot, and teach a sometimes smug mother that only He is truly in control.

10

A GLIMPSE
OF GRACE

At first glance, I thought the letter was a mistake. The signature was unfamiliar, and the opening paragraph referred to an incident that I couldn't recall.

But as I read on, my memory slowly returned. I remembered unanswered phone calls, terse words, anger, and disappointment. It had all happened more than a year ago, a slightly unpleasant business transaction that had frustrated me at the time.

At least, that's all it had been until the letter arrived. The letter explained a little about the background of the situation, offered no excuses, and simply asked for forgiveness. The writer was a man I had met once, talked to on the telephone a half-dozen times, and would probably never see again. Yet he had taken the time and cared enough to write and ask for my forgiveness.

In the midst of a busy day, the simple letter stopped me cold. How easy it was for me to criticize, condemn, complain. How rarely did I ask for forgiveness in the wake of my actions.

As I pondered the letter, I realized how important asking for and offering forgiveness really are. It's not just a way to salve our consciences or clean the slate. The act of forgiveness takes us out of the mundane and puts us in touch with the holy.

We can't say the words, "Will you forgive me?" without giving up pride and control. We can't say, "Yes, I do forgive you," without letting go of the hurt and self-protection that comes from being the victim of pain. We become extremely vulnerable when we forgive, and in doing so, we catch a glimmer of what God's grace is all about.

"Forgiveness is love's way of dealing with life's injustice," says Lewis Smedes, in *Forgive and Forget*. How often we struggle with the unfairness of life, wondering why others triumph at our expense, or why cruelty seems to abound in our world. As mothers we must explain these realities of life to our children at a very early age.

Yet, we can also begin to learn and teach the concept of grace as we forgive one another.

After a particularly long and trying day recently, I was short-tempered with my son. Finally he asked, "Mommy, why are you angry?" I began to explain that he needed to listen more carefully, obey my instructions, . . . and then I realized that the problem was really with me.

The act of forgiveness takes us out of the mundane and puts us in touch with the holy.

So I sat down beside him and told him it was wrong for me to be angry. Then I said the words, "Will you forgive me?"

At first I thought I was pushing the limits of a three-year-old's understanding. But he seemed to ponder the idea for a moment, then he wrapped his arms around me and said, "I forgive you." In his words and touch I experienced once again the healing power of love.

11

AN
IMPERFECT
EXAMPLE

I pressed the doorbell and waited for my neighbor to let me in. Inside the house I heard the chaotic sounds of three-year-olds in full birthday party frenzy. *Brave woman*, I thought, realizing that at this time on most days, the children would have been home taking naps.

The door had barely opened when I heard a familiar squeal. "Mommy, Mommy," called my son. "Come see what the clown made for me," he said, holding up a blue balloon twisted into the shape of a dog. "Oh Mommy, I love it," he beamed.

Children ran through the house as I made my way in to greet other parents and thank the hostess. My son headed off to join the boys who were playing on the swings in the backyard. I watched as he carefully guarded his treasure. There was no need to warn him that balloons could break. He wasn't taking any chances.

After a few minutes of small talk, I went outside to find Chase and saw him playing with a boy who looked slightly older. Chase was proudly showing him his balloon. Suddenly I saw the boy grab it from Chase's hand, throw it on the ground and stomp on it until there was nothing left but a shred of blue rubber.

Chase's first reaction was shock. He stood looking for a moment at what had been his precious balloon dog, then he picked up the pieces as if there might be some hope. Then he began to sob silently.

I was holding him in my arms by the time the tears began to flow in earnest. His body heaved as he buried his face in my shoulder and whimpered. "Why did he do that?" he asked me over and over.

I felt tears in my own eyes as I held my son and tried somehow to ease the cruelty of the act. As he cried and cried, I hugged him and prayed that his life would be spared as much pain as possible along the way. I wanted so much to protect him from the cruelty of other children, the madness of the world, the many threats to his well-being. I wanted to explain enough to comfort him, but not so much to scare him about the future.

"It was very mean of him to do that," I began simply. "He *is* a very unhappy boy and wants everyone else to be unhappy, too," I tried to explain to my sweet, gentle son, who wouldn't even step on bugs.

I wanted so much to protect him from the cruelty of other children, the madness of the world, the many threats to his well-being.

"I loved that balloon," Chase said. "He's a mean boy, isn't he Mommy?" he asked, looking at me with his tear-stained face. I continued to stroke his hair as the crying slowed a bit.

Just then, the boy walked by with his mother and began taunting Chase with "Cry baby, cry baby." I felt anger begin to overwhelm me. "Now Honey," his mother said. "That's not nice." I wanted to hit both of them as the boy kept up his jeers and his mother smiled at me as if to say, "Boys will be boys."

I tried again to explain the situation to my son. "I know it made you feel very sad when the boy broke your balloon. Some people are very mean. Even some children are very mean."

"You mean like bad Indians and pirates?" my son suggested.

"Sort of like that," I said. "But you don't have to be like that because you are a very special boy. And you make Mommy and Daddy and Jesus very happy when you are a good boy and are nice to other children." I was doing my best to moralize, despite my own feelings of anger.

Out of the corner of my eye, I saw the boy approaching again. But before he could say anything, Chase pointed at him and said, "I hate you. You broke my balloon."

Part of me wanted to stop him. But part of me wanted him to fight back, too. I wanted him to learn to defend himself against the assaults of others. I didn't want him to be so vulnerable to pain that he was constantly bruised by life.

I wasn't sure if the encounter had been good or bad for his moral development until later that night as he lay in bed discussing the events of the day with me. "I tried to be a good boy," he said, "but that boy made me so mad." Then he added, as if to summarize, "I would never smash anyone else's balloon because it would make them feel too sad."

I kissed my son goodnight and hugged him for a long time. As I did, I prayed once again for his protection. For myself, I asked for wisdom, forgiveness, and understanding. There were so many days when being a mother pulled me in different directions. I prayed that God would show me the way and give me the strength to raise this special little boy. And I asked him to work in my son's life, even when I am an imperfect example.

12

RUNNING THE RACE TOO FAST

Standing on the sidewalk in front of our house, I waited impatiently for my son and his babysitter to return from their walk. *They said they'd only be gone for a few minutes,* I thought to myself. Chase's dinner was getting cold.

Finally I saw their two heads coming over the hill down the block, Chase wearing his bright red baseball hat, Doris with her dark curls. "Hurry up, guys," I shouted, waving to get their attention. They waved back without increasing their pace.

Remember Doris's leg, I told myself. It was easy to

forget about her disability. She cheerfully went about her work, sometimes joking about her "wooden leg." When she wasn't much older than my son, Doris had been hit by a car and the doctors in her native Peru had amputated her leg. She'd grown up with an ill-fitting prosthesis that caused her to limp.

As Chase and Doris came closer, my restlessness changed to concern. *Something was wrong. Chase was limping, too.* "Chase, are you all right?" I shouted. "Did you hurt yourself?"

My fears eased a bit as Chase let go of Doris's hand and ran to me as fast as his strong little legs could carry him. "Mommy, Mommy," he said as he began to tell me all the news of his walk down the block. I was too busy examining his leg to listen to his description of birds and leaves.

Chase continued to reassure me that he felt fine, and as Doris caught up with him, I questioned her, too. "Oh, you mean you wonder why he was walking like that," she said, finally understanding the cause for my concern. "He always walks that way with me."

"But why?" I asked.

"So we can be alike," she said, trying to find the words in English to explain.

Then I realized there was nothing wrong with my son at all. In fact, he was healthier than his mother, especially in his view of life. Despite the fact that he could walk, run, and jump, he chose to limp beside Doris, slowing down, taking time, walking with her rhythm, not his own.

How rarely I slow my pace for others. And when I do, it's with a certain impatience that shows I could be going faster if it weren't for them. Even worse, I often justify my whirlwind pace with words like *stewardship, responsibility,* and *commitment.* I attempt to sanctify my approach, even as I push past others without taking the time for a kind word or an open heart.

I often justify my whirlwind pace with words like stewardship, responsibility, and commitment.

As I reflected on my son's example, I was reminded of the pattern Christ established during his short life. In the Bible, Christ is rarely portrayed as being in a hurry. He's usually walking, not running. He's often sitting—by a well, on a hillside, in a boat. He even spent forty days praying in the wilderness. And when he died at just thirty-three years of age, he was able to say, "It is finished."

Every time I think of Christ's example, I'm inspired to reconsider the pace of my own life. I keep

repeating to myself the words of Romans 12:2,
"Do not conform any longer to the pattern of this
world, but be transformed by the renewing of your
mind. . . ." And just this morning, when I was
tempted to tell my son to hurry up and get dressed,
I stopped and gave him a hug instead.

13

PRESCHOOL DELINQUENT

*I*t was the telephone call every mother fears. "I'm sorry to disturb you," the voice on the other end of the line said, "but there's been an accident on the playground."

"Is Chase all right?" I questioned anxiously, imagining the worst.

"He's resting now, but you should probably come pick him up. He has a cut on his face and he is quite upset."

"Should I take him to the doctor?" I asked, praying he wasn't hurt badly.

"I don't think he'll need stitches," the woman replied. Stitches? I thought of his tender skin, still as smooth as a baby's. "I'll be right there," I said, hanging up and rushing to the car.

On the way to the school, I thought of the television show I'd watched on safety hazards at school playgrounds. Had Chase fallen off of a poorly designed swing? Was he climbing on monkey bars that hung too high above the ground? Then I began my own second guessing: I probably should have kept him out of preschool. He was too young to be away from his mother. Now Chase was paying the price for my poor judgment.

Chase's tears had dried by the time I saw him, but the blood was still fresh on the jagged wound that started over one eye, traveled down his nose, and ended under the other eye. Half an inch in either direction, and he might have lost his sight. "How did it happen?" I asked the woman in the school office.

"Just an accident," she responded.

I was about to question her further when Chase interrupted. "Brian did it. He hit me with the lid to the sandbox."

"He didn't mean to hit you, did he?" I said, trying to find something positive about the situation.

"Yes he did!" Chase replied. "He was being mean to me, and then he hit me."

I looked at the woman in the office and saw Chase's story confirmed in her face. "Brian is going through a difficult time, and we've had some behavior problems," she said lamely.

Behavior problems? I couldn't believe Chase was the victim of a known playground felon. "You mean Chase isn't the first one he's hurt?" I asked, shocked to think that child was running around free.

Brian sounded like a delinquent, and I wondered what he was doing in the preschool I had picked for its loving, nurturing environment.

Hurrying Chase home, I tried to concentrate on comforting him, but my anger continued to grow. Brian sounded like a delinquent, and I wondered what he was doing in the preschool I had picked for its loving, nurturing environment.

The playground incident wasn't the last time I heard Brian's name. It came up with amazing regularity as Chase recounted his days at preschool:

"Brian had three time-outs today."

"Brian started a fight with Jimmy today."

"Brian took my paper during art, and then he threw my crayons."

I began to feel that Brian dominated my son's preschool life. He was the villain of the class, the child who got more attention than the others because of his bad behavior.

Finally, Chase came home one day and reported that Brian had hit him on the playground. "If he ever does that to you again, just hit him right back!" I advised, none too charitably.

Chase looked at me in shock. "But Mom," he protested, "that might make him cry." I looked at my son and realized how much my own sense of anger had begun to color my thinking about the situation.

"You're right, Chase," I replied. "I'm glad you don't hurt other children like Brian does."

A few days later, I was talking to another mother from school when Brian's name came up. "Poor thing," she commented. "He's become the victim in the messiest divorce case I've ever seen."

Brian a victim? The idea had never occurred to me. But the idea of a four-year-old torn between his parents was more distressing than his misbehavior. I felt sorry for this child whose life was being emotionally scarred by his parents.

That night, Chase and I talked about Brian.

"Nobody likes him," Chase announced. "He's always bad."

"Let's pray for Brian," I suggested. "Let's ask Jesus to help him be a better boy at school."

Chase looked at me doubtfully. Then he said, "Okay. But we better ask Jesus *and* God to help Brian, because he's *really* bad."

I tried to supress my laughter as Chase addressed his prayer first to Jesus and then to God. As he said "Amen," he looked at me with a grin. "I hope it works."

I hugged my son extra long that night, hoping he would always know how much I loved him. Then I said a prayer for Brian, too. I asked God to send an extra measure of love in his direction so that somehow he would know he was not alone.

14

THE
SPAGHETTI
GARDEN

*T*each Your Child Responsibility," the headline in the parenting magazine advised, "By Growing a Summer Garden." With the winter winds still howling outside our windows, the thought of a summer garden was more than a little appealing.

My own childhood summers had always included a sizable garden with a variety of vegetables. My father and I would plan for our crops months in advance, then nurture the seeds indoors until the last danger of frost had passed. I had loved the anticipation and the rewards of gardening. The thought of reliving the experience with my own son made me smile.

Picking Chase up at school, I could hardly contain my excitement. "Guess what," I said. "We're going to do a very special project together." I wanted to whet Chase's appetite for this wonderful adventure.

"Are we going to the toy store?" he asked excitedly.

"No, this is even better," I said. "We're going to start a garden."

"Oh, Mom," Chase whined, "couldn't we just go to the toy store?"

I realized I had some cultivation of my own to do before we ever got our hands into the soil. It occurred to me that my son did not understand the wonder of watching a seed grow into a beautiful, edible vegetable. Once he caught on to this, I was sure he would embrace the garden project wholeheartedly.

I decided to work backwards from what he understood. "What are your favorite vegetables?" I asked.

"Carrots, lettuce, and spaghetti," Chase replied confidently.

"That's good," I encouraged, "but spaghetti's not a vegetable."

"Yes it is!" Chase insisted. I decided to change the subject rather than risk an argument over this side issue. I drove Chase to a nursery and showed him the vast array of colorful seed packets. "Where are the spaghetti seeds?" he asked, confounding me with his ability to concentrate on the one thing I wanted him to forget.

"Honey, there aren't any spaghetti seeds because spaghetti is not a plant," I explained.

"Yes it is! We have spaghetti seeds in the pantry," Chase responded stubbornly.

"Okay," I said. "Let's just pick out the rest of the seeds here and worry about the spaghetti later."

Seeds, soil, and pots in hand, we left the nursery to head home and begin our garden. I had everything laid out on newspapers when I realized Chase had disappeared. A few minutes later he returned, shaking a red and blue box of spiral macaroni. "And here are our spaghetti seeds," he announced.

"These aren't seeds," I began, when an idea struck me. "Never mind, let's go ahead and plant them," I said.

Chase's interest in our garden grew as he realized that he could get his hands dirty and play with water. He carefully planted each of the vegetable seeds and watched me mark them with simple drawings of the plants they would become. Emphasizing his responsibility in this project, I talked to him about watering the plants each day. "Just don't water the spaghetti," I advised.

Every morning Chase's first stop became the little collection of pots on our window sill. "They're growing!" he'd shout as shoots began to appear. But he was concerned about his spaghetti. "No sprouts, yet," he'd say.

One morning I awakened early and beat him to our fledgling garden. Carefully, I brushed the soil aside and twisted some of the macaroni until it poked out of the dirt. Then I began making breakfast and tried to act nonchalant as Chase shuffled into the kitchen. His gasp alerted me that he had seen my tampering.

"Mom, you're not going to believe this," he said, pointing at the macaroni. "It's finally growing." I suppressed my laughter when I saw how excited he was by his discovery.

Chase's interest in our garden grew as he realized that he could get his hands dirty and play with water.

For the next two days I awakened early and twisted the noodles up a little higher. Chase became especially proud of his crop of spaghetti and began to brag about it to his friends.

One day when his grandparents came to visit, he pointed out the variety of plants and then, with great fanfare, showed them the spaghetti he was growing. Looking over his head, I winked at them, hoping they would go along with the joke. They admired Chase's gardening abilities and complimented him on the best-looking spaghetti they'd ever seen.

But the joke had gone on too long, and I needed to have a talk with Chase.

"Honey," I told him later, "your spaghetti isn't really growing. Mommy has just been making it look like it's growing so you wouldn't be discouraged."

Chase looked at me with shock and then anger. "You lied to me," he accused.

"I didn't mean to," I began, but then I realized that he was right. I had started the charade just to keep Chase doing what I wanted him to do. I had continued it instead of hurting him. But now I saw the damage I had done. "I hurt your feelings, didn't I?" I asked.

"Yes," he said. "That was mean." I waited for him to vent his anger. I deserved it.

Finally I asked, "Will you forgive me?"

"Well, okay," he said, as he wrapped his arms around me. Then looking at me with a little grin he said, "Do you think we could fool Daddy?"

I smiled at him and asked, "Do you really want to?"

"No," Chase said. "It might be funny, but it might hurt his feelings."

"You're right," I said, wondering how God could love me so much to give me a child like this.

15

THE NEW TRADITIONAL WOMAN

*Y*ou one of them career ladies?" the man sitting next to me on the airplane asked as I pulled my briefcase out from under the seat in front of me.

"I guess so," I replied hesitantly, wondering what ideas he had about women like me.

"Must be mighty exciting," he said. He shook his head as if he could hardly imagine what my life might entail.

I hesitated for a moment, wondering if I should tell him the truth or let him go on believing the myth of the superwoman. "You'd be surprised," I said, deciding to let him down gently.

The fact was that my briefcase did look professional, but inside my work papers were sandwiched between a cookbook for planning dinner and a storybook I had been reading to my son before leaving on my trip. My yellow legal pad contained two pages of my handwritten notes and several pages of my favorite three-year-old's scribbles. And the most carefully guarded telephone numbers in my address book were not for highly-placed business contacts, but for neighborhood teenagers who could babysit. My life is a far cry from the excitement the man might have imagined.

I'm often surprised by people's ideas of what it means to be a "modern woman." There's the perfume commercial which shows a glamorous woman bringing home the bacon and frying it up in a pan. And there are the stars of television shows who begin each day in designer suits, sit at clean desks, whisk off to two-hour luncheons, and get home in time to pick up their children at school. If I thought women like that really existed, I'd lose my last shred of self-worth. Fortunately, I know real women who, like me, have little in common with these fantasy characters.

I may look like someone's image of a modern woman, but inside me beats the heart of a traditionalist. I have more choices about lifestyle than my mother did, but my priorities are amazingly similar to hers. I may wear a "dress for success" suit to work, but my heart remains rooted in my home. And possibly the greatest thrill of my average week is when my son lets me sleep until 7:30 on a Saturday morning.

The distance between the public image and my private life had me totally baffled until I heard recently that a large advertising agency had "discovered" a new type of woman. They found that she looked like the contemporary woman depicted on television, but tended to act in a much more traditional way. They called her "the new traditional woman."

I have more choices about lifestyle than my mother did, but my priorities are amazingly similar to hers.

I identified with the label as soon as I heard it. I *am* aware of what's happening in the world, but that doesn't change the fact that my values are pretty traditional by most standards. I read the daily newspaper for information, but I still turn to the Bible for direction and inspiration. And I know that there are many women in the world like me.

We know that the world seems more complicated than ever. We realize that women today have to deal with changing roles. But we also believe with all of our hearts that some things never change.

16

HARK
THE HERALD
SILVERHAWKS

*I*t's going to be Christmas very soon now," Claire announced from the back seat in her best motherly voice. As the oldest and most mature member of our carpool, she often took it upon herself to remind the other children of an upcoming event.

Buckled into their seats after an active day at school, the rest of the children squirmed and squealed and talked over one another in excited tones.

"We're going to have the biggest Christmas tree in the whole world," declared David.

"I'm going to get a hundred million toys," my son said.

"We're going to decorate our house with beautiful, beautiful stars," Claire added.

I listened to their conversation and tried to keep from interrupting. I had learned that letting the children interact naturally in this strange little world of our carpool gave me new insights into their thinking, for better or for worse. Except for occasionally refereeing a dispute, I mostly listened to the discussion as the children reviewed the day's events with all of the drama that four-year-olds could muster.

But as the conversation continued I began to have an uneasy feeling that the children were missing out on the true meaning of the upcoming holiday. "Does anyone know whose birthday it is?" I asked.

"Jesus'!" they all said in unison. I felt relieved as they began to tell their versions of Christ's birth. "There were camels and sheeps and everything there," my son Chase explained earnestly, "and he was born in a . . ."

". . . manger," Claire chimed in.

Reclaiming his platform, Chase raised his voice. "And then beautiful fairies came to see baby Jesus."

"Fairies?" I asked.

"Yes," my son said emphatically. "Beautiful fairies. And they told the sheep men to come."

"Don't you mean angels?" I suggested. "Nope," my son said shaking his head. "Fairies."

I groaned as I began to question my son's spiritual education. Where had I gone wrong? Maybe I'd told him too many imaginary tales at bedtime instead of reading a Bible storybook. Perhaps he spent too much time coloring in his Sunday school class. Whatever had gone wrong, I was determined to change things before he turned into a total secular humanist.

The next day I went to the store to buy a manger. I passed by all of the beautiful china and crystal figures and settled on an inexpensive straw-covered manger and unbreakable plastic figurines. I wanted four-year-old fingers to be able to caress the baby Jesus, to relive the coming of the wise men. I wanted to teach that Christ was approachable. It seemed like such a perfect opportunity to bring the spiritual world to life.

After school I invited Claire to join Chase and me in setting up our manger. The two of them seemed delighted to be having a "manger party," and as I began to set the stage for the story of Christ's birth, I felt that a special moment was about to occur.

I had just explained that Mary and Joseph were far away from home when Chase said, "Just a minute. I have to go get something." I heard him shuffling through his toy box in the other room. After a minute he returned with his plastic igloo and toy Eskimos which he carefully placed next to the manger. "The Eskimos wanted to see baby Jesus, too," he explained. "But there weren't any Eskimos when Jesus was born," I said. "Yes there were!" Chase said. "They ate fish and used sleds," he said deliberately, trying to teach me the lesson he had learned at school.

I decided there wasn't anything terribly sacrilegious about the Eskimos seeing baby Jesus, so I let them stay. I launched back into the story patiently. Then Chase's face lit up as he had another idea. "Wait a minute, Mom," he said and ran off once again. He came back with his Silverhawk, a half-human toy I'd always found disgusting.

I had wanted so much to make Christ's birth real to my son. And the nativity scene in our family room was certainly more real than any other I had seen.

"He can help the fairies tell everybody about Jesus," he said excitedly.

That was too much. "Just a minute. There were angels, not fairies, remember? And there certainly weren't Silverhawks." Chase was too busy dive-bombing the manger to listen.

Claire, who had been patiently putting up with Chase, sided with me. "Well I'm going to help put the shepherds and the animals in the little house," she said. "No, I am," Chase said competitively.

"You can have the wise men," Claire offered. "But I get Mary and baby Jesus."

"Mom! It's my house, so I get baby Jesus, right?" Chase said, his voice rising with emotion.

"No, I said it first, so I get him," Claire said, standing her ground.

Before I could intervene, Chase and Claire were locked in battle over baby Jesus. "Hold it," I said loudly, losing my patience. I began to pry them apart. Chase, who had wrestled control of the Jesus figure, threw it across the room and in a fit of temper yelled, "I don't care about dumb old baby Jesus anyway. I'd rather play with my Silverhawks." By then we were all beginning to cry. Not only had I failed in my attempts at explaining the true significance of Christmas, I had set the stage for what seemed to me to be the most appalling display of sacrilege I had ever seen.

I sent Chase to his room, escorted Claire home, and returned to the scene of the crime to see if I could gain any spiritual understanding from the mess. I looked at the figures on the floor, the igloo on the table, and the Silverhawk still perched atop the manger, and despite my frustration, I began to laugh. I had wanted so much to make Christ's birth real to my son. And the nativity scene in our family room was certainly more real than any other I had seen.

Just then Chase walked back into the room hesitantly. "I'm sorry that I threw baby Jesus," he said. "Can we tell the story now about the shepherds and the wise men and the fai——, I mean angels?"

With his tear-stained face and sheepish grin, Chase was beginning to look like an angel again himself. As I told him the story of Christmas, he carefully placed the figures in their respective places. Then he said softly, "Is it all right if my Sky Commander comes to see baby Jesus, too?"

"Sure," I said. Over the next days I found many other toys and stuffed animals surrounding our manger, all facing the baby Jesus, some even bearing gifts. There was something deeply moving about this strange little scene in our family room. It wasn't at all what I'd had in mind when I set out to create a spiritual experience for my son. But somehow I didn't think Jesus would mind.

17

THE
BROKEN
PROMISE

*C*an we snuggle for a minute, Mommy?" my four-year-old asked as I put him to bed. "We can try," I said, maneuvering my enormous stomach into the bottom bunk.

The bed creaked in protest as I eased in next to my son. Chase moved over, placed his ear against my stomach, and listened for a moment.

"They're talking in there, Mommy," he said with a twinkle in his eye. And then, turning toward my tummy, he said, "Time to go to sleep, twins." He kissed my stomach twice, moved over next to me, and gave me a hug.

I hugged him back, grateful he was taking my pregnancy so well. I was determined to maintain as many of our routines as possible so he wouldn't feel displaced or jealous. But I knew the addition of two siblings would inevitably change things for our first-born. And that was the aspect of my double pregnancy that concerned me most. How would I ever find time to give Chase the attention he needed while attending to two newborns?

My life had always been so carefully planned. Even this pregnancy had been scheduled so that Chase would be old enough to feel secure but young enough to have common interests with his sibling. I had the feeling God was smiling at me as I held on to my illusions of control.

I thought back to the earliest days of my preg-nancy. When a friend asked Chase whether he wanted a brother or a sister, he replied confidently, "I want a brother *and* a sister." Then he added, "And a dog!" My husband, Tom, and I laughed at that, but tried to ex-plain to him that he would have a brother *or* a sister—and that a dog was out of the question.

A month later, when an ultrasound test revealed not one, but two, babies in my already enormous tummy, Tom and I were in shock. We'd never even considered the possibility of twins. We were awed by the miracle of their creation, and humbled by our own inability to determine our lives.

As the months passed and further tests were conducted, the doctor told us the twins appeared to be a boy and a girl. We were thrilled and a little sheepish as we told Chase he had been right all along. He acted as if it was the most apparent fact, and seemed to wonder why it had taken us so long to come around.

I had the feeling God was smiling at me as I held on to my illusions of control.

Meanwhile, Tom and I went through all of the worries and plans that accompany a growing family. A station wagon replaced our little Honda. We began calculating diaper usage logarithmically. At night, we'd lie in bed, discussing everything from the trivial (Should we dress them alike?) to the important (Will Chase feel left out as the twins grow up together?).

I read books on sibling rivalry and tried to include Chase in my pregnancy as much as possible. He loved to come to the doctor's office to watch the ultrasound screen as the babies moved and stretched. We were thankful Chase continued to accept my pregnancy so well. And we were even more grateful for my good health and the apparent lack of complications.

By the time I reached my eighth month, Tom and I breathed a sigh of relief. Our greatest concern had been early labor and the delivery of babies too small to survive. But ours were thriving, my doctor assured us, and were now large enough to be delivered with some confidence. Chase began to pray, "Help our twins to be born soon," to which I added an enthusiastic "Amen!"

On a hot August day, I drove to my doctor's office feeling lighthearted, despite an additional forty pounds. The babies could be on their way at any time, and I knew I needed to be ready.

What I wasn't prepared for was what happened in the next hour. I had visited the doctor's office so often that it felt like home. I joked with the nurses and then went through my usual procedures. But today was anything but normal. The nurse frowned as she searched my stomach for the tiny heartbeats.

The baby boy's was there as usual, strong and regular. But when she placed the monitor on the other side of my stomach, there was only silence.

"Wake up," I coaxed, urging my baby to move, thinking she was in an unusual position and the monitor couldn't detect her heartbeat.

Another nurse came in. She, too, searched and then, with tears in her eyes, said, "I have to go talk to the doctor."

I lay alone in the room for a long time, begging

God for faulty equipment or mistaken nurses. I prayed for a miracle. Then finally, as reality hit me, I prayed for protection for the other tiny life within.

The next few hours were filled with tests, discussions with doctors, and dozens of questions.

My husband was in a meeting and couldn't be reached. When it was time to go home, I left the doctor's office and drove for a long time, unable to face a nursery with two of everything, and my son, for whom I would have to find the words to explain the loss.

How could I make sense of something that made no sense to me? How could I ever explain that we had been given two very special gifts, but that one had been taken back before we could even know her?

When my husband came home, we cried together, feeling the loss of a baby we had never even suspected was there a few months before. Then we did our best to pull ourselves together before facing our son.

As the three of us sat on the bed in our room, we told Chase. "Remember when we told you that Mommy was bringing home two babies? Well, something happened and now we're only bringing home one."

Immediately Chase's face grew concerned. "Why? What happened?"

"One of the babies died," I said gently. Chase began to cry.

"Was it my brother or sister?"

"It was your sister," I replied, beginning to cry myself.

We spent a great deal of time crying and hugging, and trying to understand how we could lose this precious little life so suddenly. After a while, Chase looked at me and asked, "Mommy, can we have a baby sister next time?"

I hugged him and said, "We'll see, Chase."

Three weeks later I brought home a healthy, energetic little brother for Chase. Tyler's presence helped ease the pain for all of us, and I prayed that Chase would be able to forget about his little sister just as easily as he had changed his bedtime prayer from "Bless the twins" to "Bless my little brother."

Once again I had underestimated my son. Tyler was three months old when one day Chase hugged me and said, "I wish my little sister hadn't died."

I hugged him back tightly, sad to realize he still thought of her perhaps as often as I did. We talked for a while about the same questions I still asked. Then Chase added, "Should we give her a name, Mommy?"

His question surprised me. Tom and I had talked about it, but for some reason, had never settled on a name. It seemed strange to name a baby we hadn't known. And perhaps we were afraid of one more painful reminder of our loss.

"What would you like to name her?" I asked Chase. "Joanna," he answered without hesitation. "I think we should name her Joanna."

I don't know where he'd heard the name or what caused him to feel so strongly about it. But it seemed fitting that our son, who had believed in her existence before we had, would be the one to name her and give her a special place in our family.

God had used Joanna's short life to teach us many things about faith. She would always be real to us, even though we had never held her. And, as I kissed Chase and held him tightly, I thanked God for the strength and wisdom of my firstborn son.

18

ANGEL IN DISGUISE

*W*e had nothing in common. I could tell from the minute I looked over at the woman seated next to me on the early-morning flight to Chicago. She was wearing tight jeans, high heels, and a revealing blouse. Her hair was teased and sprayed; her makeup included several shades of eye shadow. She looked up from her copy of *Cosmopolitan* and smiled as I sat down.

"Where are you going this morning?" she asked in a rural Southern accent.

"Milwaukee," I replied, not wanting to start a

conversation. I had work to do on the flight, and I didn't want to encourage small talk.

"I'm going to Green Bay," she said, without waiting for me to ask.

"Nice city," I said, hoping she'd consider it the benediction to our conversation. I pulled out my briefcase and began shuffling papers.

"Fly much?" she asked.

I took a deep breath and, bordering on rudeness, said, "I guess so."

"Boy, I sure don't. Hate to fly. I'm scared of crashing. Every time I hear a noise on an airplane, I have a fit."

I looked at her again and this time saw the fear in her eyes. "Don't worry," I said, trying to adopt an official tone. "This is an easy flight, and it's a clear day. Why don't you read something to take your mind off of it?" I suggested.

She seemed to take the hint, and I went back to my work. But a moment later my concentration was broken by the loud cracking of her gum. It continued as I leafed through several pages, and I found myself rereading each sentence to the staccato rhythm of her snapping.

By the time breakfast was served I had accomplished next to nothing. "Make her be quiet," I prayed peevishly. After all, I was trying to do "Christian work." It seemed that God could be called upon to help me out.

"Nothing for me," she said to the stewardess. "I'm

too nervous to eat." She smiled at me, but didn't say a word. I could still see the fear in her eyes, but this time I noticed something else, too. There was a certain sadness about her—a fatigue that was barely masked by the bright colors on her face. The distance between us seemed to lessen as I began to sense her pain.

"Where are you from?" I asked with a sense of resignation. I knew that I was about to hear the woman's life story.

The distance between us seemed to lessen as I began to sense her pain.

She talked for several minutes about her small hometown and her dreams of a better life in a big city. As I looked at her clothes again, I realized that she had probably dressed in her best imitation of sophistication. She suddenly looked like a child playing dress up.

"Would you like to see a picture of my son?" she asked. I nodded, and she pulled out several pictures of a handsome teenager. I looked at her more closely, and decided that she couldn't be much more than thirty.

"You're so young . . ." I began, and she laughed.

"Yep. I was just a baby myself when I had him. Ran off with my high school sweetheart and next thing we knew, we had a baby."

I watched her face as she smiled and talked about the first days of her marriage. There was no pain in the memories, only happiness and wonder. But she wore no wedding ring, and I sensed that something had happened after those early years.

"He's dead now," she said abruptly. "He was such a good person. I still don't understand why he had to die." There were tears in her eyes as she told me about the car accident that had killed him two years before.

I felt tears forming in my own eyes as I listened to her describe the disbelief, the anger, and the sorrow that had driven her to a nervous breakdown following his death. "I just gave up on everything," she said simply. "Myself, other people, even God."

"Why are you listening to me talk about this?" she asked suddenly. "Most people don't want to hear about people dying. They try to change the subject. That's the hardest part. No one wanted to talk to me after a while because all I wanted to talk about was death."

"I think I understand a little bit about how you feel," I said. "Before I lost a baby I didn't like to hear anyone talk about pain. It scared me. But now I sometimes feel like I'm drawn to people who are hurting."

"Did you give up on God, too?" she asked. Looking at her for a minute, I knew it was important to tell the truth.

"I felt like he was very far away," I told her honestly. "Nothing seemed to make sense to me. But I continued to pray for one thing. I asked God to make me more open, not to let me become hard or cold."

"Did it work?" she asked.

I looked at my new friend and smiled. "Yes," I said, hugging her impulsively. "It worked."

19

A
LEGACY
OF LOVE

The only surprising thing about Grandpa Hanson's death was that it came as such a shock to me. He was ninety years old, after all. But he was so energetic that I never imagined anything slowing him down. And he was so feisty I somehow believed he'd outlive us all.

With his zest for life, perhaps he did outlive us. He packed hours into minutes with his lively banter and constant activity. He teased and joked, confronted and cajoled, all at the same time.

"Putting a little weight on, aren't you?" was the
first thing he said to me after I hadn't seen him for
nearly a year. Another time he commented on how
gray I was—after I had just spent a small fortune having my hair frosted.

But Grandpa's outspokenness was matched by his
love. "I'll still love you, even if you're as big as a house,"
he assured me. Then he snuggled up to me, standing
as tall as his five feet three inches would allow, and
rubbed his unshaven cheek against mine. That was
Grandpa's trademark—an affectionate nuzzle that left
you smarting.

Rumor has it that Grandpa actually mellowed
with age. As a young man his outspokenness resulted
in a fist fight or two. One of our favorite Hanson leg-
ends is about Grandpa driving his pickup truck in rush
hour traffic and being edged out of his lane by an ag-
gressive bus driver. Never one to back down, Grandpa
reportedly rolled down his window and told the bus
driver to get out of his lane. The bus driver pointed
out that his bus was much bigger than Grandpa's
truck, so he would go where he pleased. At that
point Grandpa's honor was at stake, so he reportedly
reached behind his seat, pulled out a sledge hammer,
and left a sizable dent in the bus before driving away.

Perhaps his temper cooled over the years, but the
speed at which he moved never seemed to change. The
mental snapshots I carry of Grandpa Hanson are all
blurred. He was in constant motion, too busy to slow
down for sentimentality. I remember him climbing

around on a three-story roof long after his eighty-fifth birthday. I see him driving his snowmobile at breakneck speed, airborne in subzero weather. If hyperactivity were a diagnosis applied to the elderly, Grandpa would have been a textbook case.

If hyperactivity were a diagnosis applied to the elderly, Grandpa would have been a textbook case.

Grandpa's boundless energy was often concentrated on spiritual matters. He was evangelical in the old-fashioned sense of the word. He never missed an opportunity to remind friends and strangers alike of their need for Jesus. True, he sometimes grabbed people by the lapels and asked, point-blank, "Are you saved?" But his doggedness paid off so unexpectedly that I sometimes questioned my own ideas about lifestyle evangelism.

It was characteristic of Grandpa that he had planned his own funeral. And it was appropriate that it sounded more like a crusade meeting than a memorial service. Grandpa would have liked it that way.

I didn't cry a great deal at Grandpa's funeral. I'd never known a man more eager to get on to the next thing—and for him, that was heaven. It was hard to grieve over the body in the coffin that looked so little like the grandfather I had known. I couldn't remember seeing him still for more than a few seconds. I don't know if I'd ever seen his cheeks smoothly shaven. And I know I'd never looked at him without seeing the twinkle in his bright blue eyes.

Perhaps I was comforted by the legacy Grandpa Hanson leaves behind. Some of us inherited Grandpa's eye color; others, his feistiness. As a child my mother often told me, "You're just like Grandpa Hanson." I could tell from her tone of voice that it was both a compliment and a curse. But I was always proud to think I resembled this man who seemed to be one of the greatest characters of all time.

And just this morning, when I went to get my year-old son out of his crib, he threw his blanket at me, impishly flashed his big blue eyes, and in a string of gibberish seemed to say, "What took you so long?" As he banged his bottle against his crib, I seemed to see Grandpa again, and I laughed and cried at the same time.

20

HAVING
IT ALL

My pile of message slips includes a pleasant surprise: My old friend Jack is in town and wants to meet over a cup of coffee.

It's been more than a year since I've seen him, and I am anxious to catch up on Jack's family, our mutual friends, and his skyrocketing career. "How about 4:00?" he suggests when I call him at his hotel.

"Great!" I reply, making quick calculations. I pick up the children at 3:15. I will just have time to drop them off, get downtown to meet Jack, and be back in time to make dinner.

But my schedule does not match reality. The

carpool line moves slowly, and the traffic is terrible. By the time I get downtown, it is nearly 4:30. I fight the frustration and concentrate on seeing Jack. When I call his room, the line is busy. *At least he didn't give up on me*, I think.

A few minutes later, Jack appears in the lobby. "Sorry. I've been on the phone." I feel relieved that I don't have to recite my mundane reasons for being late. Jack travels all over the world, and somehow, I don't think the difficulties of the carpool line will impress him.

We sit down over coffee and go through the usual questions: How's the book going? Have you seen Jim lately? How old are your kids now?

Finally Jack says, "I'm sorry I seem distracted. That phone call really turned my life upside down."

He begins to tell me about the job offer he has just received. It is the dream of any journalist—a high-profile editorial position that will give him national visibility, showcase his writing, and pay an unusually high salary. I am happy for Jack. But I feel a twinge of jealousy, too. This is a once-in-a-lifetime offer. It is a job I would love to have offered to me.

"I just can't decide if I should take it," he says. The travel will be extensive; he will be gone for weeks at a time. But that is not the problem for Jack. First, he considers its career benefits. Would this sidetrack him from his main interest? Could he make a commitment to the job for the next several years? Would he be giving up too much to leave the niche he already has created?

Finally he comes to it: "And then there's the travel. It would be hard to be away from the family so much." I nod my head, but I do not understand.

I look at Jack and see how different we really are. Yes, I would love to be offered a job like this. But no, I wouldn't even consider it. Who would drive carpool? Who would be sure a good lunch was packed? Who would be there to soothe a fevered child?

I need my family as much as they need me. I need my children more than I want fame or career advancement.

My husband does just fine when I have to be away for a day or two. But if travel were a regular part of my work, our systems would break down. And, the truth is, I would break down. I need my family as much as they need me. I need my children more than I want fame or career advancement.

The realization hits hard. Jack and I were once equals, young fast-trackers who leapfrogged our way into top positions. We were equally driven, highly competitive, and fiercely independent. But now,

I am none of those things and Jack has pulled out ahead.

Jack has a family, too. He loves his children—I have seen him bring a child on a business trip, or take time out of an important meeting to call home. But it is different for Jack. He is not a mother.

I congratulate Jack. "You're going to take it, aren't you?" I ask, seeing the excitement in his eyes. "Probably," he acknowledges. Bittersweet emotions overwhelm me. Then I look at my watch.

"I've got to go," I tell him, "I've got to make dinner." How mundane that sounds compared to Jack's news! "Congratulations," I say again, as I hug him good-bye. "I'm happy for you."

I *am* happy for him. But I am also envious of the freedom Jack has to make decisions for himself. I begin to feel a little sorry for myself as I hurry home to cook dinner. "Mommy, Mommy, I missed you," my son says as I walk in the door.

He hugs me briefly, then runs into the other room. "Close your eyes," he calls. "I have a present for you." When I open my eyes, I see he has drawn a picture of me and has written "I love you."

I stare at the crayon drawing for a long time. It is not a major award. I can't cite it on my résumé or use it to impress anyone. But today it seems more precious than anything else I have achieved.

"Why are you crying?" my son asks.

"I missed you," I say, hugging him. "And I just remembered how lucky I am to be your mom."

21

THE
DADDY
TRACK

People were shuffling slowly into the conference room. "Joe's going to be a little late," someone announced. Mentally, I reviewed the list of people needed for the meeting and tried to decide if we could get started. Less than half of them had arrived. We would have to wait.

I looked at the only other woman in the meeting and shrugged. Time was ticking away for both of us, but the men seemed oblivious. Mary needed to pick up her child at the babysitter's. I needed to get home and nurse my baby. I had timed this meeting to fit my infant son's schedule. If all went well, I'd be back just in time for his next feeding.

But all was not going well, and I was becoming frustrated. *Most of the men in the meeting could work late if they needed to,* I thought peevishly. They had wives who worried about the children. Even worse, neither Mary nor I could say anything about our needs for fear of being branded unprofessional.

The meeting was half an hour late in starting. I tried to call it to order, but two men still laughed loudly about something as I began to explain the purpose of our discussion. I started over again, looking at my watch and hoping we could move through the material quickly.

We handled the first few items, and I breathed a sigh of relief. Maybe I'd make it home in time after all.

We were about to tackle the next agenda item when a woman walked into the meeting, handed a note to one of the men, and walked out. *Must be something he needs for his presentation,* I thought. "Go ahead, Sam," I said to the man, expecting him to give his report.

"Uh, you'll have to skip me for now," he replied. "Something's just come up." He stood up and walked out of the meeting, exchanging a knowing look with the man next to him.

I tried to control my impatience. Sam was an important part of the discussion. We couldn't get far without him. We moved on to discuss a few unrelated matters for the next ten minutes. Then we were stuck without a crucial piece of information from Sam.

"Where is Sam?" I finally blurted out in frustration. The man sitting next to Sam's empty chair squirmed a little. "He'll be back soon, I'm sure."

Soon the meeting degenerated into side discussions and laughter. We couldn't adjourn until we finished our business. And we couldn't finish our business without Sam.

If it's hard for a woman to let her personal life affect her work, it must be even harder for a man.

"Could you please see if Sam can come back?" I asked his friend. As he left, I wondered if I had made a mistake. What if neither returned? This meeting was turning into a disaster, and I had to get home soon.

Sam's friend returned and said, "He'll be back in just a few more minutes."

I was at the end of my rope. "We've already waited half an hour. What in the world is keeping him?" I demanded.

"He . . . uh . . . had a little personal problem," the man replied. "His daughter bit another child, and he had to go down to the day-care center and take her home."

"Oh," I said, suddenly deflated. This was a problem I could understand. He wasn't being uncaring at all. He was being a father, dealing with the same problems Mary and I dealt with every day.

When Sam walked back into the room, I gave him an encouraging smile and asked him to give us the information we needed. In ten more minutes the meeting was over.

As I hurried home to feed my son, I realized my own attitude needed some adjusting. There's been so much talk about the "Mommy Track" lately that I'd forgotten how many men worry about their children, too. And if it's hard for a woman to let her personal life affect her work, it must be even harder for a man. I never felt the same about Sam after that day. After all, I understood what he was going through.

22

SIBLING COMFORT

I have watched the frustration building for months. At first Tyler was a novelty, a little baby whom Chase noticed occasionally. Then he became more expressive and Chase turned adoring. "He's smiling!" he would exclaim, after watching his face and holding his hand. But now Tyler gets in the way. Too young to be a proper playmate, he only bats at Lego towers or interrupts battle plans. He is a pest to Chase.

I understand Chase's frustration. I was an older sister myself. Firmly settled in my ways at the age of six, I suddenly had to share my world, my parents, even my toys, with a baby. I didn't really mind her at first. She reminded me of my dolls, so I would pat her on the back and occasionally turn her over. Once I picked her up, only to be confronted by my hysterical mother. I still remember thinking that this little intrusion would pass. She would go back where she had come from, and I could get back to life with Mom and Dad.

So it does not surprise me when Chase asks, "Will Tyler always be my brother?" He is not being unkind; he is only trying to understand what has become of the world he once knew.

What does surprise me is Chase's protectiveness of his brother. I try to wrestle a toy away from Tyler and Chase stops me. "Let him have it, Mom," he says. "I don't want him to cry." I look at my eldest son and wonder if I was half as kind to my younger sibling.

Donna and I were separated by two more years than my boys; according to books on birth order, we were so far apart that we are considered to be in separate families. I was involved in my school life when she was born. By the time she could carry on a meaningful conversation I was a teenager who refused to talk. I look at my wedding pictures and see her as a pretty young woman, but remember thinking of her that day as a child.

My little sister is a woman now. She is married and has a child of her own. An entire continent keeps us apart just as those six years separated us as children. But there are days when I take great comfort in knowing that Donna is there. We are sisters, and if I call her, we can laugh and cry and tell each other "I love you" without self-consciousness or hesitation.

When I see my boys together I feel that same comfort in knowing that they will always be brothers. They will gain something from each other unlike anything I can give them. I imagine someday that Chase, my serious son, will grow up to be a lawyer. And I fear that Tyler, the risk-taker, will go through life calling upon Chase to bail him out.

Even if I am not there, my boys will have each other.

Even if I am not there, my boys will have each other. They may fight and complain, resent each other at times, and wonder aloud how two such different personalities came from the same parents. But they will have each other.

I watch Tyler watch Chase and see the admiration in his eyes. I see Chase help Tyler, then spontaneously kiss him on the head. *"Please, God,"* I pray, *"Let them know how special this relationship is. Even if they grow apart, don't let anything divide them."* And then I pick up the phone to call my sister. I need to tell her that I love her.

23

MIDWESTERN ROOTS

A wise woman once told me that you should love your children so much that you don't try to make them into extensions of yourself. I have remembered her words, even tried to live by them most times. But I must confess to having a hidden agenda for my boys: I want them to grow up with my midwestern values.

As a child I thought living in the Midwest was boring. I longed for the excitement of the West or the elitism of the East. I did not know how lucky I was to have spent my first twenty-one years right in the center of this vast land before moving within range of the Atlantic.

Now I watch my boys and occasionally fantasize about moving them back to the Midwest where people talk to you as they make change, help a stranded motorist fix a tire, and clean up their debris at fast food restaurants.

I must confess to having a hidden agenda for my boys: I want them to grow up with my midwestern values.

My sons will soon be old enough to be embarrassed by midwestern outgoingness and annoyed by my rigid standards. Perhaps I still have time to convert them to my way of thinking.

It is difficult, however, to teach midwestern values out of their geographic home because they are somewhat tied to the weather. Winter is always coming in the Midwest, so you must keep your affairs in order at all times. People sleep on park benches in California.

Steam grates provide some comfort to those in the East. But people in the Midwest know that you can't mess with the weather. If a tornado doesn't get you, a blizzard will. Midwesterners learn very early to depend on each other.

The other principle midwesterners learn is self-consciousness. You can always tell a midwestern transplant. He is the person standing an appropriate distance back in the grocery check-out line so as to avoid bumping the person ahead of him. She is the one saying, "Oh no, you go ahead," on the chance that she did not see others who were there before her. My mother always taught me, "When in doubt, apologize." Now that's a true midwestern mother.

As a midwesterner raising two boys in the East, I know it won't be easy to instill proper values in my offspring. The children play, for the most part, with second and third generation easterners. If I'm not careful, they could become intellectual snobs. They already watch a great deal of public television.

But I know there is hope when I see my oldest son at school. He is the one at the very end of the line saying, "You were here first," and apologizing if anyone steps on his foot.

24

THE SINS
OF THE
MOTHER...

The greasy smell from the French fries began to overwhelm me as I stood in line at the fast food restaurant. I ordered a salad for myself and a children's meal for my son. "The one with Gumby," Chase said excitedly.

"No Gumby," the woman behind the counter mumbled, then blew a big bubble that burst with a bang. "That will be $4.65."

"What do you mean you don't have Gumby?" I asked as her garbled words finally registered. The woman just shrugged her shoulders and kept chewing her gum as she counted out my change and threw our lunch on a tray. My son's face fell as he realized what was happening. "But Mom," he pleaded. Suddenly his chin quivered, and he began to cry.

"You've got to have Gumby," I said foolishly, trying to plead with the woman who seemed to look right through me.

I had spent the morning running errands with my son, all with the promise that his reward would be the children's meal he had seen advertised on television. And now I was facing an uncaring woman who seemed not at all concerned that she was breaking my child's heart.

"Who's next?" she said, dismissing me. My son's sobs turned into full-scale wails.

"I want to see the manager," I demanded. People on both sides of me looked at me in surprise. The woman behind me swore and moved to another line.

Finally a young woman shuffled out from the back room. "What's the problem?" she said, glaring at me and then my son.

"We came here to buy lunch specifically because you have advertised free Gumby figures in your children's meals," I stated as unemotionally as I could.

"They're not in yet," she said. "Want your money back?"

"No, I do not want my money back," I said firmly. Then I pointed over her head at the dangling three dimensional poster with the smiling green figure. "FREE with every children's meal," the sign proclaimed. "You cannot advertise something you don't have," I pointed out righteously.

"Too bad, lady," the woman said combatively. "We don't have them, and I don't know when we're getting them. They just tell me to put up the signs, and they send me the toys." I could see I was getting nowhere. *Just wait until I let the Federal Trade Commission know about this,* I thought to myself.

"Mom, look!" Chase said before I could launch in again. He was holding up a plastic dinosaur that he had pulled out of the box. "This is really neato. This is even better than Gumby," he said.

It startled me to realize how tempting it was to put my role as protector ahead of my calling as a servant.

I felt my face turning red. The woman behind the counter looked at me with a smirk.

"Thank you for your trouble," I mumbled as I walked away with my son, hoping no one knew me.

As we sat and ate our lunch, he played happily with his dinosaur while I reflected on the humbling role of motherhood.

It didn't surprise me to realize that I had been impatient and easily angered by the encounter. No matter how hard I prayed, being longsuffering was not something that came naturally to me. But what did surprise me was how easy it was to justify anger when it was used on behalf of my child.

What lesson had I just taught my son? I wondered. Was I encouraging him to be a Christlike example to the world? Or was I reflecting a society that teaches us to "go for it" and not be a wimp? It startled me to realize how tempting it was to put my role as protector ahead of my calling as a servant.

Being a mother has changed me in many ways. But in other ways I am still the same. It is just as easy for me to sin. It's sometimes even easier to justify it. The difference is that now my sins are magnified as my life serves as a model for my children. And that's enough to send me to my knees.

Every time I see a smiling Gumby, I smile to myself. God used that silly green guy to teach me an important lesson: In my zeal to be a good mother, I can't forget to be a Christian first.

25

CHASE
AND THE
BEANSTALK

Something about the look on my son's face made me suspicious. "Did you have a nice day at school?" I asked. He nodded, then looked at the floor.

"Did anything extra special happen today?"

"No, not really," he replied.

"How's your bean plant doing?" Chase's face brightened. The kindergartners were growing bean plants, and for some reason his had shot up above all the others. For days Chase had been the envy of his friends as his plant towered over the other little sprouts.

"It's still growing," he said excitedly. "Pretty soon it's going to go to the ceiling!"

I noticed that Chase gestured with one hand while the other remained in his pocket. Suspicious, I asked if he had brought anything home from school.

"Not really," he answered, once again looking at the floor.

"What's in your pocket?"

The look of surprise and obvious guilt on my son's face almost made me smile. My son is too young to act, too innocent to hide his feelings. But I could see he was struggling with something that he knew was wrong.

Slowly, carefully, he pulled the treasure from his pocket. Opening his fist, he displayed a wrinkled bean.

I tried to catch Chase's eye, but he looked away. I could not imagine what was causing such a struggle. "Where did you get the bean?" I questioned gently.

"At school," he responded softly, shuffling his feet.

"Did your teacher give it to you?"

"Not really," Chase whispered. "It was just an extra one."

"Did you steal it?"

My words sounded harsh, but from the look on Chase's face I knew he understood. It wasn't just an extra bean. It was something he wanted and took without permission. Taking the bean was a great wrong, and Chase knew it.

"I guess so." My son seemed almost relieved by his confession. "I just wanted to grow another bean plant at home like the one I have at school."

There was more to this story, I realized. Chase's bean plant had put him on top among his peers. He had been king of the kindergarten every morning when class began and his friends saw his plant, bigger than the rest. Chase stole the bean because he loved the feeling of being ahead. It was a deeper problem than a five-year-old could understand.

Each bean reminded me of the enormous price I pay whenever my desire for approval overwhelms my commitment to obedience.

I didn't want to minimize the wrong, or overwhelm him with guilt. But this was not just about a bean. If Chase didn't understand that, it would be easier for him to cross over the line the next time.

"I know you love your bean plant at school, and I can understand why you wanted to grow another one," I told my son. "But taking something that isn't yours is wrong. It's stealing. You have to give it back."

Tears formed in Chase's eyes. "Please, Mommy, can't I keep it?"

"No, Chase," I said firmly, wondering if I was being too hard on my son. "You must take it back tomorrow. And you must tell your teacher that you are sorry that you took it without permission."

The next day Chase took the bean back to school. His teacher later told me that he solemnly presented it with the confession, "I'm sorry I stolded this bean."

When Chase returned home that afternoon, he seemed back to his old self. "Did you give the bean back?" I asked.

"Yes, Mom."

"Then I have a surprise for you." I pulled out a package of bean seeds and watched his eyes grow wide.

"Can we plant them now?" he begged.

As we planted the beans in our window garden, I felt as though I was participating in a sacrament. Every time a bean went into the dirt, I thought of the times I had cut corners or justified wrongs in the spirit of getting ahead. I wanted people to envy me, too. I wanted to be the best, the brightest, among my friends. Sometimes it was easy for me to think, *It was just a slight exaggeration.* But each bean reminded me of the enormous price I pay whenever my desire for approval overwhelms my commitment to obedience.

Chase's act of contrition humbled me, too. As our bean plants grow in the window, they remind me that sometimes the smallest wrongs draw us furthest from God. But even a tiny step back toward what we know is right can bring healing and new growth.

26

A GIFT
FROM GOD

*T*yler was not yet ready to leave the bathtub. Holding up a warm, inviting towel I tried to coax him out of the water. "No!" he yelled as he threw himself forward, clinging spread eagle to the porcelain. "No, no, no," he said, shaking his head for emphasis and refusing to look at me.

But I know where Tyler got this stubborn streak. Reaching down, I pulled the stopper and the water began to gurgle down the drain. "There," I said, pleased with myself. Tyler recognized my tone of voice. He thought that he was winning, but obviously I had found a way around him. He looked toward the drain, and seeing the water disappearing, grabbed at it. "Mine, mine, mine," he said, with rising hysteria.

---

*A*lmost *from the start, Tyler showed signs of living life to the fullest.*

This child may be a preacher, I mused, realizing that his points come in threes. But as I grabbed his wet, writhing body I knew already how unlikely a prospect that was. A street fighter, perhaps. A linebacker, maybe. But even at this early stage, knowing what I do about temperaments and phases, I cannot imagine Tyler ever bothering to explain his point of view to anyone.

We were in full scale combat now. I weigh a hundred pounds more than this child, but I could not force him into his diaper. I tried to distract him with a toy, but he shrieked and threw it across the room "Don't patronize me," he seemed to say. I tried a hug and he pushed me away. "No!" he said again, but I saw the true meaning in his eyes: "You are not my mother," he wanted to say.

Half an hour later I laid him in his crib. I was soaking wet with a combination of perspiration and bathwater. "I love you. Good night," I said, as is our ritual. He shrieked back. As soon as I closed the door, he stopped crying and began to drink his bottle. We repeat this routine most nights. He refuses to go to bed without a fight, but seems to give up as soon as he believes I am out of range. I laughed, but not so loud that he could hear me.

It is hard to remember, but there was a time when I felt sorry for Tyler. His birth was traumatic, and he was whisked away from me to be cared for by specialists concerned for his survival. When they brought him to me hours later, he seemed so scrawny and fragile that I was almost afraid to hold him.

In those early days, I worried about Tyler. Would he always be sickly, I wondered? Would he have a hard time keeping up with others? I prayed that I would not be overly protective of him, that I would not coddle him and turn him into a "mama's boy."

God heard my prayer. Did he ever. Almost from the start, Tyler showed signs of living life to the fullest. It was as if he believed, "I fought hard to get here, and I don't intend to slow down now." What he didn't grab for, he pushed out of the way. He crawled so fast that he stopped only when he bumped into walls, momentarily deflected, but never discouraged. Early on he grew tired of the slow pace of mealtimes. Soon he took over his own feeding, using two hands to stuff food into his mouth. He never bothered to walk, he only ran, leading with his growing tummy and bouncing right back from falls.

When I intervene in sibling disputes it is to protect the pride and property of my eldest, not the well-being of the "baby." He is still a baby, but we rarely call him that. We're probably afraid that he would understand the implications of the word and let us know how he felt about it.

Tyler speaks in a combination of monosyllables and grunts, expressing his wishes or displeasure in rising volume. His vocabulary consists entirely of objects he likes: lights, bottle, shoes, dogs; and commands: no, mine, go. I see no sign of an expanding vocabulary. These few words get Tyler all he wants in life, and if they don't, the rest of the family begins to offer an assortment of options instead, hoping to stave off the inevitable fit of anger, or be rewarded with his squeal of joy.

Tyler, it seems, has only two moods: anger and total joy. When I find him in his crib in the morning, he is often singing a song and banging the wooden slats, ready to burst upon the world. He squeals at the sight of dogs, jumps head first into the wading pool, and gasps with delight as he swings higher and higher. He is rarely passive. He sits contented while drinking his bottle, but only for a few minutes at a time.

Had he been my first child, I would have been completely overwhelmed by Tyler. I would have searched the baby books for symptoms of hyperactivity. Had the circumstances been different, I would have been perplexed by the intensity of his emotions. I would have had doubts about my ability to control him, and worried about his future.

He didn't just spare this child's life, he gave him a passion for living.

But the spirit I see in Tyler is truly a gift from God. Tyler is a survivor, a fighter, a conqueror. He won't be the easiest child to raise. But sometimes when he is throwing a tantrum or fighting for his way, I pause and thank God. He didn't just spare this child's life, he gave him a passion for living.

Seeing Tyler's willpower makes me want to live more boldly myself, to take risks and fight a little harder for what I believe is right. This child has as much to teach me as my firstborn. How foolish I was to think it would be any other way.

27

LOVE
NOTES

*S*o *you're* the one who started all the trouble!" the well-dressed woman said to me as I introduced myself. I looked at her blankly. Standing in the midst of our children's classroom, I couldn't imagine what she was talking about.

"The notes," she declared. My perplexed expression made her laugh. "I mean the notes in the children's lunchboxes. Because of your son, all the children have to have them now."

My mouth dropped open as I listened to her. I had no idea anyone even knew about the notes I tucked into Chase's lunchbox each day. But apparently he had shown them to his school friends, who asked their mothers for notes, too.

I thought of the times I'd wondered if the notes made any difference. I usually did them late at night before I fell into bed, or early in the morning before anyone else was awake. Blurry-eyed, I tried to draw pictures or write simple words I knew Chase would recognize.

I had no idea anyone even knew about the notes I tucked into Chase's lunchbox each day.

These notes were my way of helping Chase make it through his long school day. One of the youngest in his class, Chase struggled to keep up emotionally and physically. Sometimes I wondered if I should have held him back a year. At least at lunch time I tried to give him a little extra boost to remind him that he was special.

Now I realized the notes *had* made a difference for Chase. He felt so good about them that he had shown them to his friends. And they all wanted to feel special as well.

I went back to writing notes with new vigor. I bought special stickers and colorful construction paper to make them even more interesting. And each night, when I cleaned out Chase's lunchbox, I would find the day's note, with greasy little fingerprints on it. It made me smile to think of him reading his note each day as he ate his lunch.

One day I opened his lunchbox to find only crumbs and a half-eaten carrot. "Where's your note, Chase?" I asked him.

He looked sheepish. "Sorry, Mom," he said. "I gave it to Jimmy."

"Why?" I asked in confusion.

"Well, I hope you don't mind, Mom, but he never gets a note. So I thought I could share mine with him." Chase looked at me sideways, waiting for my reaction.

He was relieved when I bent down and hugged him. Jimmy's Mom was single and worked long hours to support her family. I guessed that spending time to write lunchbox notes was not easy for her. I was proud my son passed his precious note on to Jimmy.

"You're a very special boy," I told him.

"I know," he responded.

All I could do was laugh. I had thought that Chase needed a note each day to remind him of that fact. But not only was he keeping up with his classmates, he was even helping some of them along, too.

28

THE GOOD MOTHER

A few years ago, I picked up a book titled *The Good Mother*. Thinking it was a parenting manual, I was surprised to discover a novel about a woman who was muddling through motherhood just like I am. In fact, she even made some mistakes I had never considered. Maybe I wasn't so bad after all. . . .

Then came the movie. The role of the mother was awarded to Diane Keaton, and I fell into a funk for days. I couldn't bring myself to see a movie about motherhood played by someone so slim and chic as Diane Keaton. It seemed to confirm one of my worst fears: that being a good mother had something to do with having thin thighs. Good mothers, I also suspected, never overate, attended aerobics class daily, and always knew the registration dates for the best preschools.

Recently I heard about a theory called "good enough parenting." I'm sure it's a marketing ploy aimed at insecure women like me who know they'll never measure up. But somehow, the idea doesn't appeal to me. What does it mean to be a "good enough" mother? That your child catches cold because you forgot to send him to school with a hat, but he doesn't catch pneumonia because you *did* send him with his coat? That he grows up neurotic, but not clinically depressed? That he wears clothes that don't match, but doesn't go to live in a nudist colony?

I am content to be good enough at most things: I was happy with B's in school, I wear clothes that are almost stylish, my hair is only a year or two out of fashion. But when it comes to motherhood, I want an A. I want to be a good mother.

How will I know if I've arrived? I used to think I had the answers, especially before I had children. Now I know too much, have observed too many wonderful homes turned upside down by a rebellious child. It could happen to me.

When I meet families where all the children have turned out well, I question the mothers. "What is your secret?" I always ask. "What did you do right?" I find there are as many answers as there are types of children. "Discipline," some say. "Let them have freedom," others advise.

But I want specifics. Surely they never yelled at their children right in the middle of the supermarket. And what did they do about toilet training? Is there a limit to how long a well-adjusted child uses a pacifier? Have I already broken some important rule? Is it too late for me to be a good mother?

Part of the curse of motherhood is never knowing if you're doing a good job. But part of the joy is realizing no one's really keeping score.

I'm getting to the place in life where I realize some of the most important things have no measure. To try to quantify them is to lose some of the mystery. Study a butterfly too long and he'll fly away. Study your mothering techniques too closely, and they'll become stilted and artificial. Still, I search for assurance in my children's faces. Sometimes I find it. Other times, I fear I have failed miserably.

Part of the curse of motherhood is never knowing if you're doing a good job. But part of the joy is realizing no one's really keeping score. Those hugs and kisses aren't being tallied. But neither are the harsh words over forgotten manners. There's no cheating and no extra credit.

Fortunately, as I'm trying to be a good mother, I have a great Father to lean on. Some days I call out to him in fear. Other days I thank him for my blessings. Mostly I tell him, "*I think I'm beginning to understand now.*" For as I watch my children going their own ways, I realize how hard it is for my heavenly Father, even in his perfection, to let us grow up.

29

CONFESSIONS OF A HYPOCRITE

*Y*esterday, for the first time in my life, I considered buying a gun. It had nothing to do with the raging debate over assault weapons and hunting rifles. It had everything to do with a strange man who came to my door wanting to do yard work. Asked to wait outside, he instead walked boldly into my home, within range of my two young children. The man harmed no one. But he scared me. He made me think about all the possibilities: What if he'd pulled a knife out of his pocket? What if he'd grabbed the baby and run? What if he'd assaulted my five-year-old?

All my basic maternal instincts surfaced after the incident. I would protect my children at any cost. But what could I do to a man who was six feet tall and built like a football player?

What *is more basic, more honorable, more righteous, than a mother protecting her children?*

That's when it came to me: I'd buy a gun. I thought for a moment about where I could purchase one. I tried to remember television shows I'd seen and the various guns they had used. I fantasized about holding one in my hand, even pulling the trigger. In Rambo fashion, I would "blow away" the man before he could harm my children.

But something inside pulled me back to my senses. I had just contemplated killing another human being. I had thought of it as if it were my right. After all, what is more basic, more honorable, more righteous, than a mother protecting her children? That's when I realized that if I could even imagine killing another person, whatever the reason, something inside of me had died.

I have always been aggressively nonviolent. I urge my son to play with Care Bears instead of G.I. Joes. I turn off "Dukes of Hazzard" reruns. I stop war games in the backyard. I deplore acts of imaginary violence— but I had actually considered taking another human being's life.

I am an ordinary woman who has confronted the killer inside me. There are many suspicious-looking people in the world, and there is a part of me that wants to try, convict, and punish them with one slight movement of my index finger. *Better to get them before they get my children*, a voice inside me whispers.

Today, I face my hypocrisy. This morning I used my trigger finger to brush the hair out of my son's face and to wipe a tear from the baby's cheek. Then I used it to set the lock on the door, telling myself it is enough to protect rather than defend. I am an ordinary woman who thought she was a pacifist. Now I know better.

30

DREAMS
WRAPPED
IN PINK

*T*here is a shopping bag at the back of my closet. Tucked behind robes and winter boots, I rarely notice it. But when seasons change and I move clothes in and out of storage, I see it. Sometimes, when I am busy, I try to ignore its presence. But other days, seeing it makes me stop what I am doing and reflect on all it symbolizes.

The bag is beginning to look worn. Clothes brushing against it have given it a used look. But in fact, it has sat in the same place for nearly two years. I could move it, but I'm not sure where to put it. And moving it means I would have to face it, finally.

Sometimes, when I am alone, I seek the bag out. I make sure no one else in the family will notice my absence. Then I deliberately go to my closet, pull back the clothes, and look at it. On my bad days, the sight of it alone makes me cry.

But when I am feeling brave, I sit on the floor and pull the bag toward me. Slowly, I take out the tiny pink clothes. One by one, I examine the sleepers and bibs and sweaters. Each has a blue counterpart. But the blue versions have become stained and worn.

The pink ones remain perfect, undamaged, unworn. The only marks on these clothes are the occasional smudges where my makeup has been cried off into the soft fabric as I have tried to muffle my sobs.

I cry for the daughter I never held. But I remember her clearly. And more than that, I dreamed of her place in our family. Protected by two brothers, she would be loved and teased. The only girl, she would be spoiled by her father. My only daughter, I would teach her to be strong and soft and loving.

I wanted so much for this daughter of mine. I hoped she would have her father's wisdom, to temper the enthusiasm she might inherit from me. I wanted her to be beautiful and kind, intelligent and compassionate. I wanted her to change the world and still have time to be my friend.

Now I must be strong. I do not want her twin brother to bear the weight of her memory or the burden of my dreams. I do not want his birthday to be anything other than a cause of celebration. If I cry for her, I must cry in private. My loss cannot cause pain for my other children.

I don't know why I keep the bag. At first, in the wake of our tragedy, my husband tried to spare me pain by removing all reminders of the daughter we were expecting. But he didn't know about the bag. He didn't know about the times I found matching outfits too special to pass by. I tucked them away, awaiting the babies who would change our lives in a thousand ways.

I am not yet ready to forget my hopes and dreams.

We had no warning of tragedy, no time to prepare. Nearing the end of such a problem-free pregnancy, surely I wasn't being overly confident to plan for my two babies, was I?

I am a practical woman by nature. I am not often given to emotion. I rarely cry. I do not save the bag because I enjoy the emotion-letting that occasionally occurs when I come upon it.

But I am not ready to let her go. I am not yet ready to forget my hopes and dreams. She was my daughter for such a short time. I never held her, I never combed her hair. I never dressed her in one of the outfits I so carefully picked out for her. Yet she was my daughter, and I will not, I cannot, forget her.

31

GETTING MY GOAT

*M*ommy, Mommy!" Chase yelled, tearing into the house after school. "Look what I got today!" In one hand he carried a cardboard bank decorated with children's faces. "It's to fill with money to send to poor children," he told me excitedly. Handing me a brochure, he ran off to his room to look for some money.

I stopped to read the pamphlet, fascinated by this program that had my son so excited. It described a fundraising plan in which American children helped children in the Third World by providing animals.

Each class decided how much money it wanted to raise, and which animal it would buy. Bees could be purchased to provide honey. Chickens would offer eggs and meat. If a class of students raised enough money, it could even buy a goat for a village. The program sounded wonderful.

I was thrilled to see Chase so motivated about helping others. Lately I'd become concerned that he was becoming totally materialistic. Each time we went shopping, he begged for a toy. He only wanted to go to restaurants that offered kid's meals and trinkets. And he already had so many toys, I feared he had become completely spoiled. *Did my son even realize there were needy children in the world?*

But his enthusiasm for this new project gave me hope. Maybe he really did understand, after all.

When Tom came home from work, I could hardly wait to tell him the good news about our son. "I've never seen him so excited—even about a toy," I said. "Isn't it wonderful?" Tom and I spent a quiet moment enjoying the rewards of parenting before Chase burst into the room.

"Dad! Do you have any money to send to poor children?" Chase asked. "I want to fill this bank up to the top." Tom searched his pockets for change and I took a dollar out of my billfold to help Chase in his campaign.

"Thanks, Mom," he said. "Maybe we'll be able to buy a goat now."

As the days went by, Chase's enthusiasm never

diminished. He asked everyone he met for spare change and even emptied his gumball machine. By the time he was ready to take his bank to school, there was hardly room for another penny.

I was thrilled to see Chase so motivated about helping others.

"Your teacher is going to be very proud of you when she sees how much you collected," I told him. "And just think how happy those children will be when they get their goat."

Chase looked at me with the look little boys give their mothers when they are feeling superior. "No, Mom, you're confused," he said. "The children get the money in the bank. Then they send *us* the goat. Can I keep him in the backyard?"

My mouth fell open. It dawned on me that Chase envisioned this fundraiser as an animals-by-mail program, not as a way to give to the poor. Chase had been begging for a dog for the last year. He must have decided this school program offered him the chance to finally get a pet. I tried to find a way to let him down gently.

I pulled out the brochure and showed him the pictures of the poor children. Then I tried to explain that they didn't have any food to eat. "When I send them this money, they can go to McDonald's," Chase pointed out. I started over again.

When a disappointed look came over his face, I thought I had finally gotten through to him. "Okay, Mom," he said resignedly. "Now I get it."

As he left for school, he looked at me with a little twinkle in his eye. "Do you think maybe they'll send me a little chicken instead?"

"Just kidding, Mom," he added when he saw my face fall. As he ran off to school, I marveled at the resilience of children. For days Chase had been expecting to receive a goat. Now he knew he wasn't getting anything in return for his bank full of money. But as he left for school, he was humming a little song. Maybe he was starting to understand the joy of giving after all.

32

THE GHOST OF CHRISTMAS FUTURE

*T*here were less than two weeks left until Christmas, and I still had so much left to do. I had planned my Saturday down to the minute. Up before the rest of the family, I had breakfast on the table, a shopping list prepared, and was ready to take advantage of the early hours at the mall. If all went well, I'd be home by noon.

My husband ran out to the hardware store for a quick purchase, while I got the kids dressed. By the time he returned, I'd be ready to leave. Everything was right on schedule. I began to mentally rehearse my path through the stores.

The sound of the doorbell interrupted my thoughts. *Tom must have forgotten his house key,* I thought. I ran to open the door and was greeted by a blast of cold air. Framed in the doorway, the morning sun to her back, was an elderly woman. A wool hat was pulled down on her head and a handknit scarf circled her neck. She stood shivering as she clutched her pocketbook.

"Can I help you?" I asked, wondering if she was collecting for a charity so early in the morning. But I saw no envelope or clipboard. And besides, she looked too old to be trudging door to door in the subfreezing weather.

"I'm so sorry to bother you," she began. "But my car has broken down." She pointed at a car parked in front of our house as if to verify the story. The car looked old, too, but well kept. "Would you mind if I use your phone?"

"Come in," I said, realizing that I had kept the poor woman outside while I listened. "It's freezing out there."

"I was hoping to get an early start on my errands," the woman explained. "But the car began to stall out, and I thought I'd better pull off of the busy road and call the towing service."

I pointed the woman to the telephone and noticed how efficiently she called her car service and gave directions for them to find her. There was a spirit of independence about her that seemed incongruous with her soft pink cheeks and obvious age.

"Thank you," she said, as she hung up the phone.

"I'll just wait in my car for them to get me," she said as she walked to the door.

"Wait. You'll freeze to death out there," I said, my concern for the woman making me forget my plans. "Just wait inside until they come," I suggested.

"I don't want to be any bother," the woman insisted. "You're busy with your family." By then the baby had begun to squeal and my older son was asking, "Who's that? Who's that?" over and over again.

I sat the woman down in the living room and offered her a cup of coffee and the morning paper as I attended to my sons. "Thanks so much," she said. "I didn't get a chance to read the headlines this morning."

I hope I still care about reading the headlines when I'm her age, I thought, as I went back to dressing the children. I looked at my watch and wondered where Tom was. I was beginning to fear my carefully planned schedule would be derailed.

Tom walked in the door just as I finished with the boys. He looked at me quizzically and then nodded toward the living room. "This poor woman's car broke down, and she's waiting for the tow truck," I explained. Meanwhile, the boys ran into the living room and stood staring at the woman. She reached out first to Chase and shook his hand with a smile. Then she picked up Tyler with the ease of someone accustomed to handling babies. "What cute children," she said. They seemed to warm up to her instantly.

"What's wrong with your car?" my husband asked, and my stomach tightened. "Maybe I can fix it," he offered, before he could see the look of warning on my face. My husband, the amateur mechanic, could get lost in an engine for hours. He had already promised to watch the boys while I shopped. But he couldn't do that while fixing a car.

"How kind of you," the woman responded, and I felt guilty for my selfish thoughts. "When my husband was alive he always took care of the car. But he's gone, and the children are grown and moved away, so I'm on my own now." She said it with no self-pity or bitterness, almost with a sense of adventure. I looked at this woman again and wondered what there was about her that made her seem so special. She was so old, but so feisty. *I want to be like her when I get old*, I thought.

Tom went outside with the woman, while I tried to entertain the children. I looked at my watch and realized the mall had already opened. I imagined the parking lot filling up, the lines forming at the cash register, the aisles becoming clogged with shoppers. Frustration began to build, and I found myself resenting this woman's intrusion into my Saturday. *Maybe I should have let her sit in her car*, I thought peevishly.

Half an hour passed before Tom and the woman returned, both shivering, and my husband smudged with grease. "I've almost got it!" he said triumphantly, ignoring my pained look. "Just need another tool!"

It was noon before the car was fixed and the woman thanked us as she went on her way. "Think I'll just go home now," she said. "I'd hate to try to do any shopping at this point." I knew what she meant, as I prepared to venture into the worst of the pre-Christmas frenzy, a sense of frustration overwhelming me.

My shopping trip was a disaster, and I felt anxious for the next two days. *How would I ever get everything ready for Christmas?* I wondered.

In my hurry to get things done for Christmas, I'd forgotten to appreciate how much I had.

Then a small pink envelope arrived in the mail. I ripped it open without a thought and was stopped cold by the words. It was a thank you note from the woman. But it was more. "Never forget how lucky you are to have your family," the note advised. "Watching you, it seemed like only yesterday that my family was all together. God bless you."

I felt tears forming in my eyes as I read her words. In my hurry to get things done for Christmas, I'd forgotten to appreciate how much I had. This unexpected visitor, who had ruined my plans, had also given me a new perspective. Someday I might be like her, alone except for my memories. I wanted them to be filled with love, not shopping lists.

33

HOLDING ON TO INNOCENCE

The sun had just risen over the Chesapeake Bay when my son shook me awake. "Time for our adventure," he announced. I groaned, glanced at the clock, and tried to think of something that would convince him to let me sleep a little while longer.

"It's too early. The crabs are still asleep," I replied in a groggy but authoritative voice.

"But Mom," he pleaded. It was guilt that finally drove me out of bed. I had promised him an adventure that morning, a time when he wouldn't have to share me with his little brother. I could see the excited look on his face even with only one eye half open. Sitting up in bed, I tried to quiet Chase down as I pointed to his once-sleeping father.

Pulling my clothes on, I went through a quick checklist of gear: crab net, bucket, towel, string, bait. My stomach turned at the thought of the raw chicken necks in the refrigerator. *Why are crabs attracted to such disgusting things?* I asked rhetorically. Then I laughed to myself. Part of what attracted my son to this "sport" was the chance to watch me cringe at the sight of raw chicken hanging on a string.

Walking down the hill on our way to the water, Chase chattered excitedly. "Do you think we'll catch lots and lots of them, Mom?" "Will you tell me if we catch a baby and have to throw him back?" "Can crabs jump out of the bucket and come get you?"

I listened to this little manchild with amusement. One minute he bragged about his ability to catch crabs, even though he had never gone crabbing before, and the next, he was afraid. Last night at bedtime, he had prayed, "And please help me be very brave when I go to catch crabs." He clutched my hand as we walked, and I knew he was a little nervous about this unknown experience. But he trusted me, so I promised him I wouldn't let any crabs "come get him."

I laid our towel out on the dock in a little ceremony meant to help him appreciate our adventure. Out of the bag came string and dripping chicken pieces ready to attract our prey. We sat on the towel, eased our lines into the water, and waited.

Less than thirty seconds had passed when Chase asked, "Should we check our lines, Mom?"

"No, Chase. You'll feel a crab pulling on the line."

Another thirty seconds passed. "You think we need to find a better spot?"

"No, Chase," I replied. "We just have to be patient."

I realized then that my son did not understand that most people catch crabs in order to eat them.

Chase shifted on the towel and peered into the water. "I sure don't see any crabs in there."

Suddenly, his string moved. "Mom, help!" Chase yelled, nearly dropping the string. He grabbed me as I reached for the net. "We got one," he announced to the world. And then, "Careful. Don't let him get us."

The net wrapped around the Maryland Blue, and I lifted him out of the water, legs thrashing, mouth still holding the chicken. He fell into our bucket with a plunk, opening and closing his claws menacingly.

Chase stood back, eyeing him suspiciously. "Are you sure he can't get out?" he questioned. I assured my son of his safety. "Maybe we should put him back now so he can breathe," Chase said. I realized then that my son did not understand that most people catch crabs in order to eat them.

We caught two more crabs before we decided to show them off, then throw them back into the bay. As we carried our bucket back to the cottage, Chase began to play one of his favorite games. "Mom, why did God make trees?" he asked.

"To give us shade and wood," I replied.

"Why did God make chickens?"

"To give us eggs and meat," I told him. "And crab bait."

"Why did God make crabs?" he asked, and I realized that he suspected the worst.

I debated the answer as I saw the look of concern in his eyes. Then divine inspiration struck: "So we could have an adventure," I said. My son smiled at me as he took my hand, holding on to innocence just a little while longer.

34

A FEW
GOOD
MEN

I am interviewing one of the most successful men in the world. I have not judged him for this honor; even if I could recognize it, I would not be able to rank success. His publicity materials have done the job for me. They proclaim him brilliant, energetic, and forward-thinking.

I have not known the man for more than half an hour, but I am allowed to ask him questions more personal than I would discuss with a close friend. Being an interviewer gives one permission to probe and poke at a stranger's life, bordering on rudeness, all for the sake of making the subject seem more human.

But I am not just a writer. My curiosity about this man goes beyond who he is to what I can learn from him. I am the mother of two boys. Perhaps one or both of them will be successful, too. I have dreams like any mother of watching a son sworn in as president of the United States, or reading his name in *The Wall Street Journal,* or cheering from the sidelines as my boy makes a touchdown at the Super Bowl. I think, perhaps, that there may be something I will do right or wrong that will influence my boys' success. Maybe there is something I can learn from this man that will help me.

For more than an hour, I listen to this famous man tell me about his accomplishments. He has fought for his ideas and triumphed. He has honors and degrees and awards. His name will go down in history. I can understand why he is a success, but I struggle to make him seem human. There is so little warmth or vulnerability in this man that I am tempted to turn off my tape recorder and simply write the interview from his résumé. He gives me all of the facts, but I search for feelings.

Finally I get up the courage to ask him what I want to know more as a mother than as a journalist: "What is your mother like?"

"What?" he stammers, thinking he has misunderstood.

I repeat my question, and he looks at me as if to say, "What does she have to do with anything?" As a mother, it hurts me to see this response. I try again.

"A man as successful as you must have had a head-start," I explain. "Was there something in your childhood that helped you want to work so hard, to risk so much in order to succeed?" I want to hear him say that his mother loved and supported him, that she encouraged but never pushed. I don't want to learn that his parents were extraordinary, but I want to know the key to raising a successful child.

I don't want to be the mother of a son who values touchdowns over tenderness.

This brilliant man is thrown by my simple question. He searches his memory, but comes up with nothing. "They were good parents," he says, without a hint of warmth. He sits silently until I ask him my next question.

We talk more about his work, and then I conclude

the interview. I have the information I need to write an article, but I have not learned anything about being a better mother.

I am driving away, replaying the questions and answers in my mind, when I suddenly realize more than I will tell the readers of my story. This is not what I want for my boys at all. I do not want to raise sons who will have honors but no heart. I do not hope for accomplishments without kindness. I want to raise boys who will be loving men, who will change the world compassionately, perhaps without fanfare. I don't want to be the mother of a son who values touchdowns over tenderness.

It is a realization that gives me hope. I may not know how to raise achievers, but I do know how to love. Perhaps I can be the mother of successful men after all.

35

OPEN
DOORS

*I*t was a beautiful late spring day, and I was driving down the street with my car windows open and not a care in the world. Suddenly, I saw something that made me nearly stop. It was a lawn strewn with possessions. Tacked to a tree in the middle of the yard was a sign that said, "SALE."

I am rarely attracted to other people's castoffs, but this time I was intrigued. Off to one side was a baby crib. Next to it was a highchair and stroller. Then I saw the windup swing and walker. The owner of these goods, a woman in white slacks, looked younger than I and too thin to have borne many children.

A car behind me honked, and I sped up a little, staring in my rearview mirror. *How did she decide?* I wondered. *What was it that made her sure enough to sell all her baby gear?* I was so compelled to ask her, I almost pulled over to the side of the road. I wanted to look into her eyes and ask, "How can you be so sure you will have no more children?"

I wanted to look into her eyes and ask, "How can you be so sure you will have no more children?"

She looked so confident, so happy. Wasn't she mourning this passage? Or was she one of those women who is so certain about the number of children she would have that she counted the days until the end of her childbearing years?

Chances are, I will have no more children, either. Just this morning I watched my two boys snuggling and felt that my family was complete. My youngest, who loves the attention we lavish on him, would be squeezed between two siblings. My oldest, who so willingly shares the spotlight with the baby, would get even less from us if there were another.

And yet, I cannot shut that door completely. Some days I even open it up a little more and ask, "What if . . . ?" Wouldn't the boys adore a little sister to tease and protect? Wouldn't another boy mean even more possibilities for backyard games and indoor mischief?

Baby clothes tumble out of boxes in our attic. Maternity dresses sit nearby. I know my husband covets the storage space, but he doesn't say anything. It is a practical question with an impractical answer. I am not yet ready to decide.

We've made this decision before. Twice, to be exact. The first time, we were wonderfully naive and foolishly confident. It was time, we decided, to become a family. We never imagined how we would change in the process.

The second time, we thought we understood what we were getting ourselves into—but we were wrong. The expected addition of a sibling became the promise of two. And then, just as we had adjusted to the news, we had to readjust to only one baby and the loss of another we would never know.

So now we realize that the decision carries more weight. We understand how much more there is to lose. But we also know how much more there is to gain from another child.

Some days I ask myself, "Is there anything more meaningful to do with my life than produce children?" These are the days I imagine having five or six. This is total fantasy, and I know it. My patience is tested by two. And yet, I am healthy, and we have a happy home, and I could probably get more organized. . . .

Other days, I remind myself that if I had another child, he or she would have an old lady for a mother. I would be downright elderly by the time the child graduated from college. *It's not fair to put a child through that,* I think.

A few months ago, my husband seemed to warm up to the idea of another child. I had just taken our children across the country by myself, and I could not imagine how I ever became the mother of two, let alone how I could willingly consent to a third.

But then the trip was forgotten, and I began to notice babies everywhere. By then Tom was no longer in the mood. "Things are just settling down," he pointed out. I could not dispute his logic.

Now we both agree in principle that it would be foolish to consider growing our family more. And yet I still wonder. . . .

I long for the decisiveness of that woman who cast out all her baby paraphernalia. What confidence! But I'm not there yet. Children are still an open-ended promise for me. I love the ones I have too much to close my life to more. I am not ready to say I will never again hold a baby to my breast, await that first smile, or even drag myself out of bed in the middle of the night.

Besides, maybe a friend will need those spotted maternity dresses or stained baby clothes. I should probably keep them around—just in case.